FINDING MY WAY
IN MILWAUKEE

A Guide True Story Book

FINDING MY WAY
IN MILWAUKEE

Jennifer Jill

SCHWIRZER

REVIEW AND HERALD® PUBLISHING ASSOCIATION
HAGERSTOWN, MD 21740

Copyright © 2007 by Review and Herald® Publishing Association

Published by Review and Herald® Publishing Association, Hagerstown, MD 21741-1119

Review and Herald® titles may be purchased in bulk for educational, business, fund-raising, or sales promotional use. For information, please e-mail SpecialMarkets@reviewandherald.com.

The Review and Herald® Publishing Association publishes biblically based materials for spiritual, physical, and mental growth and Christian discipleship.

The author assumes full responsibility for the accuracy of all facts and quotations as cited in this book.

This book was
Edited by Penny Estes Wheeler
Cover art by Matthew Archambault
Design by Trent Truman
Electronic makeup by Shirley M. Bolivar
Typeset: Goudy 13/16

PRINTED IN U.S.A.

11 10 09 08 07   5 4 3 2 1

R&H Cataloging Service
Schwirzer, Jennifer Jill, 1957-   .
Finding my way in Milwaukee.

    1. Adolescents—United States.   I. Series: A *Guide* True Story Book.
II. Title.

818.6

ISBN 978-0-8280-1913-2

Dedicated to

*my niece, Rebecca McGuire,
and my nephews, Timothy, Shawn,
and Gavin McGuire.
Auntie Jen loves you!*

Chapter 1

Awww, Mom, we can't move!" I whined, clenching my hands into fists. "I love Aurora! All my friends are here."

"I know it's hard for you to leave," my mother said kindly, "but you're father has been transferred. You'll make new friends in Wisconsin, Jennifer."

Wisconsin! That sounded like another planet. All I had ever known was Aurora, Ohio—a cute little town where everyone knew everyone else's dog. And now, according to my mom, we were moving to Wisconsin at the beginning of the summer.

"Mom! Why does dad need to be *transferred?*" I wailed. "What could be better than living here?" I looked at her with puppy eyes.

Mom was quiet and gentle, but she made it clear that there was no way to change the plan. Finally I put my face in my hands and sobbed until tears ran down to my elbows, which were propped on my knees, which then became soaked with tears, which finally ran down my legs and onto the floor. I sure knew how to have a good cry.

"Then I want to be *buried* in Aurora!" I wailed, determined to get my own way somehow.

"That's fine, Jennifer. I think that can be worked out," Mom said, smiling a little.

And with that I fled to my room and flopped onto my bed, sobbing into my pillow until it was as soaked as a car wash sponge. Just about the time I had cried my last cry I heard the floor creak outside my room and saw the tall shadow of my dad.

"Jennifer, your mother tells me you're not happy with the idea of moving." In answer, I simply sniffed and looked at him with my puppy eyes. "But did you know that the family will be staying at a lake this summer?" he asked me. "It's called Big Cedar Lake, and it's about an hour from where we'll be living. You'll get to spend the summer waterskiing, sailing, and swimming. How does that sound?"

I sniffed again and nodded a little. Dad smiled and gave me one of his big wet smooches, then walked out of the room and carefully closed the door. Somehow, bit by bit, I drifted off into la-la land where, for a brief time, I could forget all about the move.

Every day from then on was all about packing. Boxes, boxes everywhere! One morning a big van came and swallowed up the innards of our house, leaving it empty and forlorn. Meanwhile, our two cars were bulging with extra boxes, suitcases, and miscellaneous madness. Our dog, Sootie, pranced around, yipping and panting. When our two-car caravan finally rolled out of the driveway, my dad was in the front car with my little brother Scott, and Mom followed with we three other kids and the dog. I think Dad knew that having my hyper little bro in the car with us would have been a little too much for ol' mom.

Driving through Chicago was the worst part of the trip. Since we didn't have a cell phone, if we lost Dad there wasn't a whole lot we could do except pray we'd find his car again. Dad drove at warp speed through the roads and highways and didn't look back to see if Mom was behind him. She kept up most of the time, but the tollbooth fiasco was one exception.

Mom wheeled up to the tollbooth window, fumbling in her purse for the right change. Sootie tended to have a neurotic reaction to people in uniforms, and the tollbooth man was no exception. Sootie began barking like a psycho.

"Don't mind him!" Mom shouted through the open window. "He's just a little ex—

Just then a furry black missile propelled itself out of the window. "SOOOOOTIEEEE!" Mom screamed, flinging the car door open. The honking Chicago cars piled up behind us as she chased the dog around the car. Finally Dad appeared and the two of them cornered Sootie. Grabbing him by the collar, Dad picked him up like a bag of beans and tossed him back into the car with us.

"Kids, you hold that dog next time!" he shouted over the noise.

It was good to see smoggy Chicago fade into the distance. Big Cedar Lake wasn't far away, but our stress levels were already maxed out. When my little sister began to yelp, Mom almost lost it.

"Kids! *Kids!*" she yelled to the back seat. "Simmer down! Kristin, you stop squealing!" Mom couldn't see that my older brother Stu was poking my baby sister in her chubby, ticklish little tummy. She was only 5, and she couldn't keep quiet—especially when being poked.

"Simmer down" was Mom's way of telling us that we'd get in trouble if we didn't behave *pronto*. She never spoke in inappropriate ways, but she used weird little words that made us sound like we were a potful of potatoes.

When the car rumbled onto a gravel driveway Stu lost his interest in tormenting Kristen and looked out the window instead. "Is this Big Cedar Lake, Mom?" he asked. He was always gathering information and making sure of the facts.

"I . . . I think so," she mumbled. Just then we rounded a corner and saw a big sign that read:

Cedar Lake Cottages
Owner: Robert Deetmeyer

"Yes, this is where our cottage is," Stu told us with

authority. "Dad said that Robert Deetmeyer was the owner." Being the oldest, he liked to be in the know about things. I gazed at the big sign, and noticed that it looked kind of beat-up. I had been hoping the cottages would be a bit on the *elegant* side of summer cottages. I was getting older and more prissy—not the tomboy I'd been a few years before. But as our cars skidded into the little driveway in front of our new place, I realized I was in for a summer of spiders.

"Mom, this is really not what I had in mind," I huffed, but before I could get a response, my little brother Scott shot out of the other car, wildly waving his fishing pole.

"Cool! Cool!" he shouted. "This is a cool place!"

We picked our way out of the car and began lugging bags up the front steps of the house. Suddenly, as if she'd been hiding there, a teenage girl appeared out of the tall pines. She was a little older than I, and wore a big, loose sweatshirt over jeans.

"Hi! I'm Jan Deetmeyer," she said.

"Oh, yes, you must be Mr. Deetmeyer's daughter," my mom said, putting out her hand.

"That's right," Jan said, shaking Mom's hand and taking a sideways glance at my brother Stu. She wasn't what you'd call a pretty girl, with her long, stringy hair, pimples, and droopy blue eyes. But she had a ready smile and a "cool" way about her.

"My dad told me that a family with four kids was coming to the lake. I told all the other kids that are staying here for the summer, and they all want to meet you," Jan said. She kept her eyes pretty much nailed to Stu, probably because he was a cute boy just about her age.

"So where are all these kids?" Stu asked, looking away from Jan into the distance.

"They might be down by the lake or at the snack bar," she said. "I don't know. We'll have to find 'em." Then Jan turned to all of us and said in a loud, announcer-type voice, "I'll be giving a tour of the area to any who want to come."

"Cool!" Scott shouted, "I want a tour. Cool." He said "cool" way, way too often.

"Can I go, Mom?" I asked, not wanting to be left out.

"Yeah, I think I should go too," Stu said casually. "You know, to find out where things are."

"Have Kristin back before dark," Mom said, waving us on. She was glad to get some time alone with Dad.

Jan led the pack of us with long, confident strides. Although her eyes were on Stu most of the time, she seemed to want to be friends with me too. Kids spilled out of the cottages and began walking with us. There was something magnetic about Jan that drew the pack of kids to her as if she were an ice-cream truck. Jan breezed through the various paths and piers, giving the grand tour as if she owned the place. Even Stu, who was strictly there to gather information, was paying attention to every word she said.

What I didn't know at the time was that this remarkable girl would bring a remarkable amount of trouble into my summer.

"First of all, there's a snack bar over here where you can get Dilly Bars. Once you eat them, look at the stick. You might win a car," Jan told us. Then she bought a Dilly Bar right then and there, offering me my first delicious bite—vanilla ice cream frozen into a circle, dipped in crunchy chocolate. She plowed through the bar like an old pro, finally licking the stick to see if she won the grand prize.

"Awww, 8%$@! I didn't win," Jan moaned, as if swearing was a normal way to talk. I felt a little jolt go through my body when she swore, almost as if someone had hit me in the chest.

"What did you say?" Scott asked, wide-eyed and innocent.

"She said she didn't win," I chimed in, hoping Jan wouldn't swear again.

But she did swear again. And again and again. As we walked through the cottages at Big Cedar, then down to the lake and out to the end of the pier, Jan kept a running speech going, with swearwords hitting the air every few seconds.

In fact, every time Jan opened her mouth that entire summer—provided parents weren't around—a string of swearwords would flow out as naturally as bubbles from a fish. I was amazed at how fearless and tough she was. She wrote on her sweatshirts and cut her own hair without asking. But then, if she had asked her dad, he would have said, "Sure, Jan, do whatever you want." That seemed to be his parenting philosophy—to give his daughter absolute freedom.

One day Jan and I were at her dad's house talking, and her tough-girl shell cracked a little. She told me about her parents' divorce and how sad it made her feel. "Now my dad is married to another woman," she said, "and I really don't like her. I live with my dad every summer and go home to Mom for the rest of the year. I guess it's OK, but it would be really cool to have a family like yours . . ." Her voice sort of trailed off into nothing.

A family like mine? With all the rules, and the strictness of my parents compared to hers? I couldn't see what it was she longed for.

« « «

One morning in August, Jan came to the cottage to say goodbye. "I'm going back to my mom's," she said. "I have a couple of weeks to shop for school." We agreed to write to each other, and to be friends forever and ever and ever. But I knew deep in my gut that I might never see her again. The letters went back and forth for several weeks. I used all the words I had learned from Jan so that she'd see me as a tough girl like her. Unfortunately—or maybe I should say fortunately—my parents found one of the letters. They called me into my room that day.

14

"Jennifer, we found this letter," Dad began.

"And we were heartbroken at the language you used!" My mother finished his sentence.

"I think Jan Deetmeyer probably influenced you to talk this way"—Dad was shaking his head—"but your mother and I don't approve."

"It's just not ladylike," Mom said, "and it reflects poorly on you."

I felt as if each of their comments peeled a layer off the hard shell I had built up, and all my tender feelings were being exposed to the air again. Tears poured down my face, and deep, wracking sobs welled up from my heart. Then my father, as if to drive the last nail into the coffin of my bad language, made an unusual request.

"Jennifer, I want you to pray out loud right now."

Pray out loud? How embarrassing. But Dad wasn't giving me a choice about it. He began reciting a prayer I learned when I was small.

"Dear God, I pledge myself to thee . . ."

I recited with him:

"to always do the best I can,
and do it lovingly.
Bless my home and all my friends.
Protect me while I play.
And help me to remember
To say this every day. Amen."

And with that, my parents were gone from the room, leaving me alone with God, my conscience, and a few summer-cottage spiders. The swearword spiders had been scared off for good by a simple prayer and some really good parents.

That wasn't the last of the woes I caused Mom and Dad. I was soon to be introduced to a whole school full of tough, rough kids. There was no going back to my quiet, safe Aurora now. I was in for a wild ride in Milwaukee.

Chapter 2

School started before we moved into our new house in Milwaukee, so we drove from Big Cedar Lake for the first few weeks. I had daydreamed about what it would be like. Of course my fantasies all featured me sailing into instant popularity, getting tight with a lot of fun friends, and meeting really neat boys.

"Oh, Jenny. You look *lovely*," my brother Stu said in a sickly sarcastic tone as we got in the car that first day of school. I had worked hard to put my outfit together. It was a feminine-looking dress, like something I'd wear to church.

"Leave me alone," I said, giving him a little push. As much as my big brother annoyed me, I could tell he was as jittery as I was about being a new kid. The car was silent as we drove. Scott and Kristin dozed, and Stu and I ignored each other. Finally we turned into the driveway of Bayside Elementary School.

"You'll make friends quickly," Mom said, as if to settle the butterflies in our stomachs. "I'm sure they're a nice group of kids."

If only she had known!

Stu and I were in the upper grades, so we got off at the bigger building while Scott and Kristin went to the smaller one. Stu and I, being in different grades, also went our separate ways. I felt so lonely that even my sarcastic brother would have been a comfort.

"Students, this is Jennifer Wilson. She's just moved to the area from Ohio. I'd like you to say hello and welcome her to our class," my new teacher announced. Mrs. Manns was a pretty blond woman who looked as if she might have come from Hollywood.

I felt a classroom full of eyes on me. In my fantasies of my new classmates they were eager to meet me, and clustered around asking questions. But clearly those dreams weren't going to be fulfilled at Bayside Elementary. Several students kind of grunted, a few said hi, and then they all turned back around. I saw one girl point to my dress and nudge her friend. They both snickered. And that was it for my welcome to Bayside.

At recess I wandered around alone, trying not to be noticed. This was hard because my clothes were so different from everyone else's. Many of the girls in my class wore revealing outfits that looked like they had come straight off the catwalk. Suddenly my church dress seemed like a loud, bad fashion statement. What I didn't see was that it wasn't really my fault that the kids were unfriendly. Somehow, trashing other people was their twisted way of feeling better about themselves.

There was nothing that made this clearer than the way they treated Gary Abramson. Gary was short and fat and talked in an adultlike voice. He was mega book smart, but also emotional. Kids treated this part of his personality like a button on a toy, pushing Gary's cry button until tears came out—push-cry, push-cry. Then they'd run away laughing hysterically.

One day our assignment was to give a speech about after-school activities. "Now students, we will make our presentations on extracurricular activities," Mrs. Manns said cheerfully. "Which of you prepared something?" No hands went up for quite some time. Finally Tim Greer's hand shot up as if he'd had a flash of genius.

"Fine then, Tim," Mrs. Manns said with a nod. She seemed a little skeptical. "Come up and tell the class what kinds of activities you engage in after school."

Tim was a thin, homely boy with a reputation for rowdiness. He walked slowly to the front of the classroom and stood with a slight smirk on his face. He cleared his throat.

"For my after-school activity, I started a club," he began with a straight face. "It's called the 'Pound Abe Club.'" With that, Tim's lips parted in a fake grin showing his crooked, yellow teeth that he probably never brushed.

Little snickers broke out across the classroom as everyone realized that "Abe" was Gary Abramson, and that the "Pound Abe Club" was all about beating up Gary.

"The purpose of the club," Tim continued as if he was giving a real report, "is just what the name of the club says—to pound Gary Abramson as he's walking home from school. We wait in the bushes as he rounds the corner from the skating rink to Brown Deer Road. When he's close enough, we jump out and grab him—"

"All right, Tim!" Mrs. Manns cut in finally. "That's not funny. Sit down."

The snickering hung in the air for the rest of class in spite of glares from the teacher. Gary seemed extra alone on the playground that day, strolling around trying to look as though he didn't care.

"Abe, you're such an idiot!"

"Hey, fatso!"

"The 'Pound Abe Club' is gonna get you!" came the taunts. In response Gary laughed too loudly as he tried to seem indifferent, but I heard tears and fears in the middle of his laugh.

I didn't stand up and defend him, but my heart felt like it had been poked full of holes and the blood was draining out. Being considered a loser myself, I had a soft place in my heart for other losers. I began a little ritual of praying for Gary whenever I thought of him or saw him—something I had never done before in my life.

"God, please help Gary Abramson," I would say.

"Everybody hates him even though he's not a bad person—just short and fat and geeky. Please help him find some friends." I felt as if my prayers for him would improve the lives of losers the world over, and so improve my life, too.

Gary had one more big embarrassment before the kids finally left him alone. This time it was the teacher who shamed him. One day he was being a little too disruptive in class. I would have cut him some slack, but Mrs. Manns decided to make an example out of him. "Gary, do you want to be disruptive? Then we'll give you the floor right now," she had said in her you-really-annoy-me voice. "Come up here right now and tell us all about why you are passing notes and distracting the other students."

Gary tried to act as if he thought it was funny, but the redness on his ears and his hunched-over posture told a different story. Being reprimanded by the teacher was too much for his sensitive soul. Wearing a manufactured smile, he slowly dragged his chubby body to the front of the room.

"Well, let me see . . ." he began, his voice shaking. Immediately kids began to snicker. "Uh . . . I passed notes because . . ." Then his voice cracked and his eyes filled with tears. He tried to pretend that he was scratching his forehead in order to think, but really he was trying to cover his red eyes.

"Let's see . . ." he sighed, trying to hold back. But like a wave breaking through a wall, his emotions came tumbling out. His eyes began to spill big, round tears.

A wave of giggles rippled through the room. Tim Greer sighed, "Oh, Gary, don't cry!" and then laughed loud enough to get a glare from the teacher.

"You may sit down, Gary," Mrs. Manns said. "And let that be a lesson to all students who wish to disrupt the class."

I couldn't understand why even the teacher seemed determined to pick on Gary. Didn't she know the students would torment him all the more? I kept praying for him until a few weeks later when the kids seemed to leave him alone. I wondered if maybe there was a God up there after all who appreciated the fact that I cared about someone else. Maybe the kids left Gary alone because God told them—in some Godlike way—to *back off*. Or maybe the novelty of bashing Gary Abramson had worn off. Either way, things got a little better for ol' Abe.

« « «

Another thing God had done was to give me a cute little sister. She was only 5, but she had soft brown eyes that seemed to understand my woes. One night late she crept into my room. "Jennifer, I can't thleep," she whispered.

"Come in my bed. I have room," I said. Kristin jumped under my flowered bedspread and fuzzy blanket. "Kristin, are the kids in your class *nice?*" I asked.

"Thure, they're nith," she said in her lisp.

"Well, mine aren't," I confessed. "Sometimes I feel so lonely."

Kristin didn't know a lot of fancy words, but she did have the cutest little hands. She circled me with her chubby arms and began to pat me on the back like a mother burping a baby. I didn't burp, but I did feel better. Family is a great thing when you're going through hard times.

Her comfort was much needed. The next day was one of the worst of my life.

"OK, time for recess. In exactly 25 minutes line up for me," Mrs. Manns ordered. It was 10:30 a.m. A herd of hyper kids burst out of the door onto the concrete playground. I was wearing my favorite blue-and-green-striped dress. I knew I'd probably spend the recess alone as usual, but it didn't matter so much anymore. I'd made a few friends and hoped to make more. Plus I was wearing my favorite dress, and that always makes a girl feel good.

As I walked toward the kickball court I noticed Wendy Potter walking straight toward me, followed by a group of girls. Wendy was tall and skinny with thick glasses and a loud voice. She was a strange mix of ultrapopular and major troublemaker. I had seen her fearlessly mouth off to teachers and even the school principal. Each time she'd come back laughing in victory.

"Hey, Wilson!" Wendy called, coming close and hovering over me. I looked her straight in the eye and didn't like what I saw. If it had been written out it would have read "mean little lie."

"What?" I asked, almost hoping she'd say something nice, like "Wanna play kickball?" or "I have some extra Fritos in my lunch. Here—take 'em." But that was just my dream of acceptance talking.

"We wanna talk to you!" Wendy's voice was too loud for a normal conversation, which was a very bad sign. When Wendy got loud, someone usually got hurt. This time I had a funny feeling it was going to be me.

"Yeah. We wanna talk to you," came an echo. The girls standing behind Wendy stepped up into my field of vision. Tracey Burnt was a quiet kid who followed Wendy around like a shadow. Jodi Gallan was a great athlete and a straight-A student, but she had a mean edge. Laurie West looked and talked like a boy and normally hung around with much older kids. Mary Chesterton was usually seen walking around with her boyfriend. Mary was mature for her age, and dressed in a way that made the boys take notice. Standing there together, they formed a wall of bullies.

"We wanna tell you that we're not happy about somethin'!" Wendy yelled.

"Yeah!" came the shout from the wall of bully girls.

"What?" I asked, totally psyched out by now. I'm sure fear was written all over my face.

"You're trying to steal Jim from Mary," Wendy bellowed for the whole world to hear. Jim Simpson was Mary Chesterton's cute, blond-haired boyfriend. He was kind of sly and smirky, his eyes in perpetual slits. I was afraid to even have one word of conversation with him.

"Yeah!" the herd yelled.

"What?" I said in total amazement. "I never even *talked* to him!" Now Mary herself stepped forward.

"Yes, you did. You came along when I was standing next to him—"

"And you stepped in between them." Wendy finished Mary's sentence.

"I did not," I said, but it seemed like my voice was so weak that the only place it could be heard was inside my head.

"So you're coming with us," Wendy yelled, grabbing my arm and walking me toward the baseball diamond. I didn't fight back because it wouldn't have made any difference. There were eight or nine of them, and only one of me. Once at the baseball diamond, they circled me like a pack of wolves. Wendy gave the first shove, and the others followed her lead. It didn't take long before I lay on my back in the dust.

"What's going on?" I heard a male voice in the crowd and saw one of the guys standing there with a ball in his hand. Another and then another joined the crowd, curiously looking down at me as I cringed on the ground. Soon there were a few dozen kids standing in a circle around me, all watching Wendy and her wolf pack close in on their victim.

The girls seemed to be taken over by demons. Flailing and shouting, they did things I don't even like to talk about. It was the most humiliating experience of my life. And the hardest part was that it was all so *phony!* I had never even spoken to Jim Simpson. But they had to convince themselves of a lie so they'd have the push they needed to fulfill their need to control someone else.

The abuse seemed to last forever. Finally they left me there in the dirt to pick myself up and go back into the school. The bell had rung, and students were flowing into the courtyard, lining up at the door. A few girls I didn't know well came to my side and helped me brush off. Exhausted, I finally sat on a bench in the courtyard. For a split second I caught a glimpse of myself in the big plate-glass window. My hair was matted with dirt and grass, and my face was swollen from crying. Seeing myself all messed up made me start crying again. How would I ever live this down? Shaking and exhausted, I joined the line of kids and tried my best to pretend that nothing had happened.

Mrs. Manns handpicked Wendy Potter, Mary Chesterton, Jim Simpson, and a few others from the crowd of kids at the door. She allowed the rest to go into the classroom. As the line marched by, I overheard her lecture:

"I know what you kids did, and I don't like it!" she shouted. "If I see this kind of thing again, you'll all go to the principal's office." I suppose Mrs. Manns thought that if she actually punished them they might be even meaner to me. She let them go back to class.

After that, each morning as I walked from the bus to the school, a pack of kids led by Wendy were waiting at the door to follow me in. "There she is!" they'd say. "Look at her stupid shoes and her ugly dress." Day in and day out they taunted me as if they wanted to break me down. Night after night I'd toss and turn in my bed, dreading the next day at school.

Even though at the time I didn't really know Jesus, He helped me through those sad months. In the middle of crying myself to sleep, I would feel a kind of peace in my heart. I somehow knew there was something better than the crazy little world at Bayside Elementary School. Someday God and I would meet heart to heart, but it wasn't quite time yet. I needed a little more preparation. Maybe He knew that I had to see the other side of life—what it was like to be popular. That was coming next.

Chapter 3

Scrrrape, scrrrape, scrrraaaape was the sound coming from my ice skates as I glided around the Bayside skating rink. Circle after circle I flew, hardly looking. I had made a few friends, but none of them had shown up at the rink tonight so I skated all by my lonesome. My favorite rock song was blasting over the loudspeakers until it was cut off with:

"THE RINK WILL BE CLOSING IN FIVE MINUTES! Please come into the lodge and collect your belongings." It was Joe, the man with a motorcycle jacket who ran the skating rink. Joe wasn't afraid to yell at kids who didn't cooperate, so I flew straight toward the lodge.

I screeched to a halt when I saw who was at the door with his buddies. Benjy Wallace! My least-favorite person. Benjy was a short kid with thick glasses who made up for his small body by having an extra-big mouth. Little and loud, he tried to use words to shrink people down to a manageable size. The last thing I wanted was to be shrunk by Benjy. I snuck over to the rack that held my shoes, hoping to avoid his eyes, but no such luck.

"Hey, Wilson!" A sneering voice cut through the hum of people.

"Leave me alone," I said.

"Hey, Wilson! You're not paying attention to me," Benjy jeered. Rolling my eyes, I turned to see him standing there in all his big-mouth glory surrounded by a few faithful followers. "You're ugly and I can't stand you!" he yelled.

"Leave me alone, Benjy," I muttered, trying to turn away.

"I said you're ugly, Wilson. And I can't stand you." He had big, crooked teeth that his orthodontist was trying to corral with braces. He seemed like one big wire-filled mouth and a pair of thick glasses perched on the end of a little stick of a nose. Every time he yelled, a string of spit would fly into the air between us. Such a charming fellow, really.

"Benjy, bug off," I said, but not with enough volume to be heard over his yammering.

"Wilson, I want you to know that I think you're . . ."

"KID, LEAVE HER ALONE," an older male voice boomed out. It was Joe, the rink attendant, looking tough with a cigarette dangling out of his lips and greased-back hair. Benjy whipped around to see the man standing over him, then slunk away to the door after giving me one last vicious glare.

"OK, I'll leave her alone," he said, "but she's UGLY!" And with that, Benjy darted into the night with his goon squad following him.

After such an encounter, one would think there would be a permanent distance between myself and Benjy Wallace. But it wasn't that way. Less than a year later he was asking me to skate at the very same rink where he told me I was ugly. The amazing part wasn't that he asked me to skate—*it was that I said yes!*

The ritual went like this. Boy asks girl to skate. If girl says yes, boy and girl skate, holding hands, circle after circle, until the song is over. Girl then goes back to her friends to giggle about it, and boy goes to his friends to brag about it. Boy asks girl again the next night. Eventually boy and girl skate the whole night, circle after circle. Boy then pulls out his ID (as in "identification" on a silver bracelet) and says, "Wanna go with me?" (as in go steady). Girl says yes (usually). Boy and girl skate together every night, all night, until they break up, at which point girl gives back boy's ID.

"Uh, Wilson, er, Jennifer, wanna skate?" Benjy asked one night, approaching me in the lodge as I sipped hot chocolate.

"Oh, sure," I said. Benjy had grown at least an inch, so that he was only four inches shorter than me instead of five. I don't know why I said yes, except that I liked being liked. Did I like him? Well, he had gotten more civilized from the time he said I was ugly—which isn't saying much—but I can't say I *liked* him. For me, skating with a boy was a status symbol rather than a sign of feelings.

"Hey, I wanna ask you a question," Benjy said after several nights of circling around the rink. I could feel it coming.

"What?" I asked.

"Wanna go steady?" he asked, his ID bracelet clenched in his mitten.

"Sure," I said.

And with that Benjy flashed me his jingling bracelet, which I wore for our entire relationship of about three weeks. Yes, after a very rocky start, I had the honor of being Sir Benjamin Wallace's first girl-friend. *And* the first girl in the sixth-grade class at Bayside Elementary School to go steady. But I admit it was a political relationship.

One week we went skiing with a group. Benjy was trying to be a gentleman and ski with me, but he was so much better than I was. He sailed down the slopes, wooshing and slicing back and forth in between people, while I snowplowed down, tur-tle-slow.

"Try this!" Benjy called, modeling a slalom across the hill.

I drew my skis together to attempt it, but as soon as I moved forward, I tipped over like a glass of water on a mattress.

Sssscccccrrraaaaaape! Clatterclatterclatterclatter. My skis flew in all directions across the snow.

"Hey, watch it!" one skier yelled, dodging my fly-ing pole.

"You idiot!" another screamed while just missing my skis.

I looked up at Benjy, my hat half off my head. This was a telling moment. Either he would scorn me like the others, or be a real prince and help me up. He stood there for a moment with his poles firmly fixed in his mittens and dug into the snow. I could tell he really didn't want to be seen with the worst skier on the slopes, especially when she was scattered like chicken feed across the hill.

"No offense, Wilson, but I wish you could ski," he said, his big teeth flashing a smile. He was nice enough, but when he reverted back to calling me Wilson I knew our relationship was over. The moment of truth had come. We weren't meant for each other, and we knew it. We opted for a no-fault breakup, and called it quits.

Too bad Benjy didn't keep up with his niceness. It seemed as if the whole school got infected with gossip about me. I didn't mind losing Benjy, but being rejected and then backbitten was a flashback to so many other hurts. The cool kids had found another reason to put me down.

« « «

The good part of all this was being free of Benjy. The bad part was that now all the boys at Bayside thought of me as the "going steady" type. Add that to the fact that I had a very hard time saying no. That meant that the only way to avoid the boys was to run away—not easy in a grade school where there were only about 100 students.

The first admirer was Todd Lemington. Todd was tall and lanky with a crop of wiry red hair. A friend of his came to me, saying, "Todd likes you, you know," which led me to carefully avoid eye contact with Todd from then on. But the rumors kept swarming like bees around a slice of watermelon.

"Todd Lemington is in love with Jennifer Wilson."

"Jennifer Wilson is in love with Todd Lemington."

"Todd and Jennifer are going steady."

"Todd and Jennifer are getting married."

The longer they rumbled the more stupid the rumors became.

"Todd is going to ask you to go steady," a classmate finally said. "I sit next to him in math, and he told me so." How crazy was that! He had absolutely no proof that I liked him. There was no way he would risk his ego with so little hope. Or so I thought, underestimating his cluelessness.

It was during math class that he popped the question. The funny part was that he used my last name to make his proposal. Walking toward my desk, he bent down to get on eye level with me. I shied away as if he was going to hit me—and hit me he did, with the question "Wilson, will you go with me?"

"No!" I rolled my eyes as kids snickered. I hated to hurt his feelings, but he sort of shrugged and walked away as if he didn't care. He wasn't as hurt as

I would have been. In fact, he wasn't hurt at all. So much for my tenderhearted pity for the underdog. The underdog cared more about following through on a dare than a relationship with me.

Was Dennis McCabe also acting on a dare or a bet from his buddies? I don't know to this day, but he went to even greater lengths in self-humiliation to grab my heart's affections. Again the rumors made the school buzz with the snickers of boys and girls who wanted a piece of the gossip. And again I cringed at the thought of wounding the delicate feelings of a member of the male species. But alas, I had no interest in Dennis.

One day there was a tremor in the crowd of classmates. "Dennis is going to ask Jennifer to go steady," the murmurs vibrated through the classroom.

"Hey, Jennifer," the girl next to me whispered. "Don't go near Dennis during recess. He's going to ask you to go with him."

"Really?" I asked, "Did he tell you that?"

"His friend told me," she said, "and basically everyone knows."

The overwhelming evidence was that it was so. Soon I would be sought after by another lovelorn male who thought I was too kind to say no. *It's true! I hate saying no!* I thought. *The only solution is to run when I see him coming.*

And run I did. It was study hall period and kids were gathered in the library and hallway. Out of the corner of my eye I saw Dennis approach. He was medium-tall with brown hair and big, green eyes that were now riveted on me.

"Here he comes!" someone said, stating the obvious.

I fired up my feet and ran. Flying out of the library and into the hall, I sprinted toward the door. Certainly, I thought, if Dennis saw me dusting him he'd take that as a no.

I overestimated his smarts.

"Go, Jennifer!" kids started to shout as if at an Olympic competition. As I peeled past one classroom after another, kids lined up on both sides of the hall like spectators at the Boston Marathon. "Go, Jennifer! You can beat him!" they shouted. My adrenaline was high, and I was flying at top speed. Unfortunately, Dennis was flying too.

"Go, Jennifer!" they yelled, jumping up and down and pumping their arms. I rounded the corner and lunged toward the door. Dennis was on my heels, but as he rounded the same corner his feet slid out from under him and he fell flat. Glancing behind me, I saw him skid across the floor, arms and legs splayed in all directions. It was a total wipeout, a devastating end to a wild chase. Now I had enough of an advantage to shoot out the door and out of sight.

I think he finally got the hint.

Things calmed down after that. The going-steady proposals ended, and rather than being known as the girl who couldn't say no, I was known as the girl who sure could run. I was relieved to be free of boy problems. Now I could focus on what I really liked, such as basketball and oil painting.

I decided I didn't really like grade school romances. Circle after circle we went around, until we were dizzy. It was kind of like a competitive sport for us, a way to show off without really thinking about what a relationship would take. And it usually ended with a big wipeout and a lot of people laughing.

OK, I'll admit that it felt really good to be accepted, to be wanted, especially after being the loser of the century. You see, God wasn't central in my life yet, so I tried to get all my heart needs from people. That turned life into a roller-coaster experience. After being so unpopular, I thought that being popular might fill the empty space inside of me. But I would soon find out that even stars get lonely.

Chapter 4

The Bayside Elementary School talent show was coming, and all the performers were polishing up their acts. I wasn't in the show because I just couldn't figure out what my talent was. "I can't do anything well," I complained to my mom who was always there to pick up the pieces of my heart.

"Why don't you perform with Dexter?" she asked. Dexter was my dummy—literally. I had performed with him for a talent show in Aurora. He was a cute little guy with a string in his back that I'd pull to make his mouth open and close. I'd talk in a high voice without moving my lips to make it seem like he was talking. During the talent show in Aurora, I memorized Mom's clever little scripts, and the performance went flawlessly. Hundreds of people cheered and clapped, making Dexter and me an overnight sensation. But that was when I was 8. Now I was 11, and wouldn't be caught dead with a dummy.

"No way, Mom," I said, rolling my eyes. "The kids would laugh me off the stage."

"Well, what about reciting a poem?"

"No offense, Mom, but these kids are a little to urban for 'Animal Crackers and Cocoa.'" That was a poem I'd memorized and recited for another Aurora talent show. "I just don't think I have any talent for performing, Mom. I'll stick to drawing."

"I don't think that's true, Jennifer," she countered. "You sing well, and you have always liked to perform for people. When you were 2 years old, you stood up on the living room table and recited 'The Old Woman in the Shoe' and 'Wee Willy Winky' for our dinner guests."

"But Mom, 'Wee Willy Winkie' just won't cut it this time," I retorted. "So I guess I'll just watch!" And with that I went up to my room to brood.

The gym was full to overflowing the night of the talent show. Sitting in the audience made me wish again that I had some special gift I could share. Something inside me wanted to perform, but then dummies and nursery rhymes didn't show who I was today. I felt like the dark stage still untouched by a spotlight.

Suddenly the light went on—not in my head, but on the auditorium stage. A student stepped into the light and spoke into the scratchy microphone. "W-w-welcome to the Bayside Elementary School Talent Show," he said, nervously reading from the paper that was shaking in his hand. "The first p-p-performer tonight is Ch-Ch-eryl Moore." Poor kid. The talent show was off to a very teeth-chattering start.

But the first performance would change that.

Dressed up like a soldier, Cheryl strode out onto the stage. In day-to-day life she was just a plain girl with long gangly arms and legs and a big gap between her front teeth. Now as she performed her baton routine, she tossed and twirled with dazzling grace. With her last toss the sparkling baton shot toward the ceiling, spinning as it rose then fell back to Cheryl who snapped it out of the air and held it to her forehead in a salute. The audience clapped and cheered.

"Our next performer is Aimee Rogers," the emcee announced, a little less nervously this time. "She will be singing a song called 'Universal Soldier,' by Buffy Sainte-Marie." Aimee stepped out onto the stage with her guitar, flinging her long, brown hair behind her shoulder as she sat down. She strummed the guitar and sang:

"He's five-foot-two and he's six-foot-four;
"He fights with missiles and spears.
"He's all of 31 and he's only 17—
"Been a soldier now for a thousand years . . ."

It was a song protesting war written by a Native American folk singer. There was a lot of war protest going on among older kids, and because Aimee was so mature she was part of it. She sang in a clear, strong voice that sounded better than the radio singers. Most of the kids in my sixth-grade class were pretty jealous of her sophistication and talent. Some of us tried to deal with our feelings by teasing her, but it wasn't convincing. She was really good, and we knew it.

For weeks after the talent show, I felt an uneasy sense that I should have come out of my comfort zone and tried performing. I didn't share my secret with anyone until the music teacher, Mrs. Rigsby, stood before the class one day with an announcement:

"Boys and girls, our school musical this year will be "Bye Bye Birdie." It's the story of a teenage pop singer who gets drafted into the war. The school choir will be singing several songs for the play, and there will also be solo parts. I hope that some of you sixth graders will try out." I don't know if I was imagining things, but it seemed like Mrs. Rigsby looked straight at me when she said that. But how could I try out when I had never sung alone in front of an audience?

"Mom, do you think I could get a part in the school musical?" I asked as I waited for her to finish cooking dinner that night. Mom was making spaghetti sauce, and its great smell wafted through the house.

"Well, you have acting in your blood," she told me, wiping her forehead with her wrist. "I was an actress when I was younger, but I gave it up because I wanted to raise a family."

"Really?" I asked, picturing my pretty mom wearing an evening gown instead of a spaghetti-sauce-stained apron.

"Yes, really. I had a big part in one play, but your dad wanted to get married before he went into the Navy, so I gave it up to marry him," she said.

"Wow, Mom! Do you wish you had become an actor instead of having us kids?"

I kind of knew how she'd answer.

"No, of course not!" She smiled at me. "I wouldn't trade you kids for the world."

I smiled back. "OK, so I have acting in my blood. But Mom, I'd have to sing for the tryouts, too."

"Your grandmother was quite a singer, you know," she mused. "So you have music in your blood as well. And Jennifer, you sing all the time around the house. I think you should try it."

"What do they judge you on?" I asked.

"Your energy level . . . whether you memorized your lines . . . expression . . . all the things you're good at, Jennifer," Mom said. "Oh, and one more thing. You have to learn to PROJECT YOUR VOICE. See, put your hand beneath your belly button," she directed, launching into a spontaneous acting lesson as she placed her hand on her stomach. "Take a deep breath, put your shoulders back, your head up, and use your diaphragm muscles to SPEAK LOUDLY."

"LIKE THIS?" I asked, letting my voice boom out.

Just then my dad lumbered into the kitchen with a newspaper in one hand. After frowning at Mom and me, he said, "What seems to be the problem?"

41

"Oh, nothing, dear," Mom chirped, "Jennifer is just learning how to act."

Dad muttered something like "Well, I think she's already pretty good at drama," and lumbered back into his "cave."

"Wow!" Mom giggled, "That was really good projection. Now, you work on that and I think you'll get a part." And with that, my was-almost-an-actor mom went back to her spaghetti sauce.

For weeks I learned my lines and one of the songs from the musical. I found that if I used my stomach muscles the way Mom said, I could get quite a lot of sound out of my little voice. Finally tryouts arrived, and I lined up in a hall full of jittery kids.

"Hey, are you nervous?" I asked one sixth grader.

"Well, yeah," she said, "but not as nervous as I'd be in front of an audience."

"I don't think very many sixth graders get parts in these plays," I said, "so we probably don't need to worry too much about that."

Just then, the moderator stepped outside the try-out room and called, "Jennifer Wilson!" I tried to look confident as I walked into the doorway. The first sight to greet me was a wall of teachers. Their faces were serious and somber, as if I had committed a crime or something. When I saw those faces, the butterflies in my stomach went from flying in circles to doing backflips. I felt like running out of the room, down the hall, down the street, into my house, and diving under my covers. But something held me there in the tryout room.

"Let's start with your song, Miss Wilson," said the moderator. Mrs. Rigsby sat perched at the piano, ready to play. I looked her way, and her fingers began to bounce on the keys. Then I belted out my song, "Put On a Happy Face."

"'GRAY SKIES ARE GONNA CLEAR UP, PUT ON A HAPPY FACE;

"'BRUSH OFF THE CLOUDS AND CHEER UP, PUT ON A HAPPY FACE.'"

Some of the teachers' faces lit up when they heard me sing. Not that I sounded pretty—in fact, I sounded a like a bicycle horn. But they had listened to one girl after another who could barely whisper, and here I was belting it out. *Finally, a girl whose voice will be heard from the stage*, they must have thought. In fact, they probably heard me the next town over.

Nervousness rolled off me as I finished my tryout. "I'm glad that's over," I said. "It was a good experience." I assumed that I'd never compete with the pretty, mature upper-grade girls, but I was glad I had given it a shot.

"Thank you very much," the moderator said, and the teachers nodded quietly. If nothing else, I had faced a fear and lived to tell about it.

The next morning my brother Stu walked up to me in the hallway. "Jenny, go look at the tryout sheet," he whispered.

"Why?" I asked.

"Just go look."

Stu was very tight-lipped, and rarely talked to me in public, so I knew something was up. I obediently walked over to the bulletin board just outside the music room where a cluster of kids were pointing and making sounds—some very happy, and some sounding depressed. I read down the list from the top where the biggest parts were:

Rosie Alvarez	Marynelle Teumer
Albert Peterson	Jim Lubotsky
Kim McAfee	Karen Marsh
Conrad Birdie	Tim Halford

"Figures," I said under my breath. "Marynelle Teumer is really smart. Jim Lubotsky is good at everything. Karen Marsh is blond and blue eyed, and Tim Halford is the star football player." I kept scanning.

Mr. McAfee	Terrance Stoddard
Mrs. McAfee	Belinda Crumbles

"All upper graders so far. I guess Stu just wanted to rub it in." Suddenly my thoughts were invaded by the sight of my own name:

Ursula Merkle	Jennifer Wilson

"Wow, I got a part!" I gasped in total amazement. "I got a part! How could this be? I got a part." I was wandering around in the hall talking to myself like a loonie tune. Then it struck me. "Who's Ursula?" I asked, wondering what I had gotten myself into.

"She's Kim McAfee's best friend. She's a gawky, obnoxious teenage girl," said one of the kids standing there. Not exactly a glamorous role, I realized, but at least it was something. Suddenly I noticed Stu standing off to the side of the group. He motioned with his head for me to talk to him.

"Do you realize you're the only sixth grader who got a part?" he asked in his hushed way, eyebrows raised. That was Stu's way of telling me he was proud of me. I have to admit that I liked impressing him—the one or two times in my life that I was able to.

But the most important impression I made was on people like Wendy Potter. It had been more than a year since the wolf pack of girls had beaten me up on the playground. None of the most abusive of them had amounted to anything in school or in things like drama, athletics, or talent shows. As I started to figure out who I was, they were all more respectful of me. I think they were pretty ashamed of what they had done.

The practices for the play monopolized my life for the next few weeks. I had only a few lines, but I was going to do it right. My first scene opened with Kim and Ursula sitting on chairs, talking on the telephone to each other with a little wall in between. We were kind of upside down with our feet in the air, the way girls talk on the phone. Ironically, Ursula talked to Kim about going steady—an issue that was all too fresh in my mind. Basically, playing the part of Ursula was easy because it was like playing me— an awkward "tween" girl, trying to figure it all out.

The big night arrived. I was nervous, but I kept remembering what Mom had taught me about projecting my voice. If nothing else, I would be LOUD. The curtain was drawn on Scene 3, and there I was, sitting in a chair talking on the telephone:

"KIM, I'M SHOCKED! YOU'RE GOING STEADY WITH HUGO, AND YOU'RE GOING TO RESIGN AS PRESIDENT OF THE CONRAD BIRDIE FAN CLUB?" There were giggles in the audience as we completed the scene, but I couldn't see anyone because of the bright stage lights. Just as well—seeing my family and the other kids in my class would have flipped my stomach.

Before I knew it, the last chorus of the play had been sung, the final curtain drawn, the very last clap had been clapped, and it was over. The actors stood in a line for handshakes, and Mom and Dad came up to tell me they were proud. Even Stu was willing to be seen with me now that I was a famous actress. He walked over with a serious look on his face and said, "Good job, Jenny."

It had been such a high time but now it was over,

and I felt like nothing really important had happened. Oh, sure, people got a good belly laugh, kids learned about acting, and a little money was raised so Mrs. Rigsby could buy new chairs for the music room. That was all great. But after all the clapping died down, there was still an empty hole inside of me. I couldn't help but wonder what my great calling in life was. Maybe it was acting, maybe singing, or maybe something else.

Chapter 5

It's a 'HI!' cheer [clap, clap], a 'HI!' cheer [clap, clap]! Let's go!

"With an 'H,' with an 'H.' with a capital 'H'!

"With an 'I,' with an 'I,' with a capital 'I'!

"With a capital 'H' and a capital 'I'

"We from Bayside say, 'HI!'"

This chant was heard around Bayside School thousands of times as the football season started. In the cool sunshine, girls clustered together on the playground to learn cheers and tumbling stunts. My cartwheel had been polished until my feet sliced straight up through the air and I struck the landing perfectly. My flip and my roundoff were also coming along well.

"Jenny wants to be a cheerleader!" Stu screeched sarcastically from his window as I practiced in the backyard one day. It was late afternoon, and the smell of dinner was seeping through screen windows, making me hungry and irritable.

"And Stu wants to be a football player!" I shot back to the faceless voice.

"And Jenny likes Jim Lubotsky," Stu cackled.

"And Stu likes Karen Marsh," I yelled. That hit home enough to button his lip for a while. It was hard to have a brother so close to my age, who knew all my secrets and wasn't afraid to tease me about them. Fortunately I had some ammo I could fire back at him.

What he said about Jim Lubotsky was true. He was tall, cute, smart, and one of the first crushes of my life. The weird thing was that he had an identical twin brother, Tom. Because adolescent crushes are mostly about good looks, crushes on a twin could get kind of confusing. To like one twin was to like the other, so I sort of wavered back and forth between the two of them. *Jim, Tom, Jim, Tom. Which one should I choose? Why choose at all?*

The Lubotsky boys would come over on weeknights to shoot baskets with Stu in the driveway. Since bucket-shooting was generally done one-on-one, the third person would sit at the kitchen table. I would conveniently plant myself there—doing my homework, of course—and lo, and behold, when Jim or Tom came in, I'd be available to chat. The twins were as friendly as they were good-looking, so conversation was easy.

Unfortunately, Jim's favorite topic was *his* crush—on another girl.

"I like a girl in my class," he'd confided one evening, "Debbie London. Boy, is she ever great."

49

Playing the therapist to a guy I liked while he worked out his feelings for another girl was harder than acing algebra, but I did pretty well. "How long have you liked her?" I asked, dreading the answer.

"Since the beginning of the year," he said. *Three weeks. That's a long time! I thought. This must be serious.*

"What do you like about her?" I asked in a counselor-like voice.

"Well, she's really good-looking," he said. *Boys are so shallow! I thought. It's all about looks.*

"Do you like her personality?" I asked, hoping he'd say no. I knew that the most exciting crushes died out when there was no substance to them.

"Her personality? I think so," he said, crinkling his eyes. *He's not even sure what a personality is! I thought.*

I hesitated before I spoke again. "Do you . . . do you think . . ." What I really wanted to say was "Do you think you could ever like ME?" But I restrained myself.

"Do I think what?" Jim asked, looking curiously at me while my mind wandered.

"Oh!" I snapped back into focus, "Do you think you should ask her on a date?" *What am I, crazy? Why did I say that?*

"Hey, maybe you're right. Maybe I should. Tell you what, next time I come to shoot baskets, I'll tell you what happened, OK?" Jim said, and with that he grabbed his basketball and headed out the door.

How dumb was that? I thought. *I'm coaching my crush through his crush. Oh well, it's better than being ignored.*

As time went on I was glad I didn't make a fool of myself by spilling my feeling beans on Jim. Feelings of attraction are like puppies inside a fence. If I had let my puppy-love puppies out, they might have pooped on the neighbor's lawn—or made Jim feel really embarrassed to talk to me. It was much better to keep secret crushes secret and keep the friendship on an even plane.

The next morning I took an extra-careful look at Debbie London as she wandered through the hall past my English class. Her dark hair flowed around her shoulders and set off beautiful brown eyes. She was so mature-looking compared to me. *When will I ever grow up?* I wondered. There was so little about me that was interesting or attractive. Except maybe my perfect cartwheel. I decided I would make up for what I lacked in beauty by being a great cheerleader.

Recess after recess was packed full of girls practicing cheers. Each girl wanted to be picked to be on one of the two 10-girl squads. The cheerleading tryouts were judged by the eighth-grade cheerleaders. They sat in a line and rated things like:

> smile
> precision
> energy

enthusiasm
voice
steps
tumbling stunts

And at the bottom of the sheet they rated the girl's general character by things like:

grades
attitude
reputation
modesty
friendliness
manners
appearance

The scoring system worked in such a way that the two highest scorers were captains—meaning leaders of the squads. The other 18 were divided into two groups, and then the squads alternated games. All the girls in my class—including Wendy Potter and her gang—were anxious to be chosen. This had the effect of reforming their bad behavior for the few weeks before the tryouts. They were amazingly talented, too. With her small, muscular body, Jodi Gallan was a born gymnast, and Mary Chesterton was pretty and energetic. I thought for sure the two of them would be chosen as captains. If I was really lucky I'd get picked to be on a squad. But I didn't count on it.

I formed a close friendship with a girl named Sue Cook. She was tall with straight, light-brown hair and an angelic face. She and I were cheering partners, and planned on trying out together. We spent hours working on our cartwheels and flips in her backyard. Then we would go into the house and find a stash of fashion magazines that belonged to her teen sisters. One day Sue showed me a picture of her favorite model.

"There it is," Sue cried. "There is that picture. Look at her. She's just gorgeous!" Sue pointed to a picture of a model with one of the most beautiful faces I'd ever seen.

"Wow, you're right, Sue," I sighed. "She is soooooo beautiful."

Of course, she was wearing plenty of makeup and had a nice hairstyle, but even considering the extras, she was special. I walked to the mirror and looked at my own face.

"Boy, Sue, I really look ugly compared to her," I said. "Too bad we all can't be that pretty."

"I guess it wouldn't be special any more if everyone looked that way," Sue said thoughtfully.

"Hey, so what?" I told her. "We can sing, right? Let's go practice our singing."

We made our way down to the basement where Sue had her music stashed, and pulled out our favorite song. We sang along with the recording, trying to sing as well as the artist, but our voices were much weaker. I said, "OK, Sue, you sing first, and

I'll coach you. Then I'll sing, and you coach me."

Sue started the song and cleared her throat. A light, sweet voice drifted out.

"Louder, Sue, louder," I coached. Sue tried to sing a little louder, but her voice was just too airy. Then it was my turn to try.

"More quiver in your voice. More quiver," she said, trying to get me to use vibrato. In spite of my grand singing debut at the tryouts of "Bye Bye Birdie," I still didn't have much confidence as a singer.

"I can't do it," I finally said. "I'm not pretty, I can't sing, and I don't think I'm going to make the cheerleading team." My insecurities were tumbling out like spilled beans.

"Yeah, I'm worried that I won't make it, either," Sue said. "I'm getting pimples, and I don't think I'm pretty at all."

It was good to know that I wasn't alone in my insecure little universe where troubles and issues flew around like shooting stars. Our bodies were changing, our feelings were changing, and our world was changing so fast we felt like we were on a rocket to some unknown planet. "Well, I'm going to try out anyway," I finally said.

"You have an advantage, you know."

"I do?"

"Yeah, the judges are all friends with your brother," Sue told me. I had never thought of that. Since Stu's friends knew me, they might be more likely to vouch for my character. Apparently Stu was my ally in this situation. For once!

"Well, I don't want to win because of connections. I want to win because I'm good," I said, "So let's finish practicing." Sue and I shot upstairs and after making a short stop in the kitchen for some cheese doodles, we hit the backyard for more cartwheels.

As I woke up on the morning of tryouts, my unconscious mind elbowed me and said, *Something big today*. Coming to my senses, I rubbed the crusts out of my eyes and sat up in bed. *Wow! It's tryout day!* I realized, and then shot out of bed like a cannonball toward the bathroom. Going through my get-up routine was an extra-careful process that morning. I brushed every crevice of my teeth, washed my face until it shone, and put my hair in extra-fluffy pigtails that would bounce as I cheered. The cheerleaders were supposed to have that "cutsie" look, so each pigtail got a bright-white bow.

The clock was a more important part of my day than ever before. Tryouts weren't until after school, so I counted each minute that ticked away before 3:00. Finally the bell rang, the kids scattered, and I dove into the girls' locker room to put on my uniform and give my pigtails one last fluff. Sue appeared next to me as I primped in the mirror.

"Hi, Jen. Are you scared?"

"Yeah, a little," I said. "Are you?"

"Well, yeah. Especially since we go first."

"First?" I cried. "We don't have *time* to get nervous!"

We changed quickly into our school colors—maroon sweaters and gray skirts—and ran into the gym to take our place in the crowd of waiting cheerleader wannabees. The panel of judges sat solemnly in a row of chairs that stretched across the gym. There was Diane and Sue Harper, twin sisters who were normally balls of giggles, but today were sober judges. Karen Marsh, who was kind of snippy and snobby, was there to turn up her cute little nose if we weren't perfect. Our gym teacher, Mrs. Stark, and Mrs. Manns were on the panel as well. Standing before my judges, I suddenly felt like the knock-kneed, all-thumbs, uncoordinated queen of klutzes.

"Mary must have rolled her skirt up," Sue said. I looked over at Mary Chesterton, whose skirt was indeed short.

"Jody has a new hairstyle," I said. Jody Gallan had her hair in a sleek ponytail and was stretching in preparation for her routine.

"Everyone is trying out," Sue whispered. "Even Wendy!" I turned around to see Wendy, who had gotten even taller and lankier, and looked a bit out of place. It seemed that every girl who could wave a pom-pom had showed up for tryouts.

"Girls!" Mrs. Stark called, "we have quite a few tryouts today, so we will begin immediately. Before you is our panel of judges. Each one has a rating sheet on which you will be rated for many things, such as your energy and enthusiasm, your voice, your facial expressions, and tumbling stunts. In addition, the judges will take into consideration aspects of character such as general attitude, grades, and your manners and friendliness. Cheerleaders represent our school, and so we want the best all-around girls on our squads. The results of these tryouts will be posted tomorrow morning on the board outside the locker room. Are there any questions?"

Mrs. Stark was met with a silence so still you could hear a dust mite walking. "Very well, then; let us proceed. Our first contestants are Jennifer Wilson and Sue Cook."

It was time to face the music. Sue and I lined up like a couple of soldiers ready for battle. Taking one last glance at each other, we smiled and began cheering our hearts out.

Only minutes later the routine we'd practiced till we could do it in our sleep was over. We sat on the sidelines and together watched the rest of the routines. I noticed that Wendy Potter was really too tall and gangly to make a good cheerleader. Her cartwheels were slow and uncoordinated, and it seemed that she didn't even know how to smile unless she was laughing hysterically at a joke. I felt a hint of pity for her, which was soon to be followed by more.

The next morning's bus ride to school seemed like it took all day. I sat on the front seat, ready to bolt out the door the moment it opened. Whirling past the other students and to the locker room, I saw Sue, who met me with a welcome smile spread across her pretty face.

"We both made it!" she cried as I arrived at the bulletin board. Then the moment my eyes fell on the list and saw my name, she said, "And you're a captain." Sure enough, the paper had two lists of names—one with Jody Gallan's name at the top, and one with mine. Reading down the list, I noticed that one name was missing.

"Wendy didn't make it." I turned to Sue as it hit me.

"The judges thought she was clumsy, plus her reputation didn't help," Sue, who must have had an inside source, explained. Just then I looked past the cluster of girls gathered around and noticed Wendy off in a corner by herself. She hid her disappointment poorly. Her shoulders were hunched and her face looked like someone had died.

A strange feeling rippled in my heart—a sigh of an emotion, achy but sweet, like a sad song. How could I be feeling sorry for someone who had beat me to a pulp on the playground? Maybe in that moment I saw through her tough-girl costume to the lonely little child underneath.

Wow, I thought, *in two years time our circumstances have been reversed. Wendy started out on top as the playground queen, trashing me like a piece of junk.*

Now I'm a cheerleading captain, and she's been left out of the loop. It was a strange lesson in how quickly things can change in a young life. I was determined to use my popularity in a more responsible way—but I had a lot to learn.

Chapter 6

"OK, cheerleaders! It's time to practice our pyramid!" I tried to yell above nine chirping voices. Being captain of the cheerleading squad had turned out to be a tough job. Sometimes, the rah-rahs drowned me out.

"Kay, Sue, Lauren, and Shawna, you're on the bottom. Then Mary, Tracey, and Megan. Then Celia and me, then Althea on top." We were practicing for the first game of the season and we had to get our pyramid right. The girls had busy little mouths, and being their boss made me have to yell sometimes. Plus I'll have to admit that I had developed an attitude problem of my own since I had become such an important person. "OK, quiet, everyone! Quiet!" I screamed. Even as they formed a pyramid, they chattered away like chipmunks—only louder.

Desperation drove me to come up with a bad idea. Being on the third layer of the pyramid, to get their attention I started jumping up and down on the girls underneath me. The pyramid broke apart right under my feet, with girls standing up and shouting.

"What are you doing?" Kay, the biggest of the girls, yelled in her booming voice.

"Yeah, you're gonna hurt someone!" Mary whined.

"OK, I'm sorry," I said, feeling really embarrassed. "Can we try it again?"

In that moment I started to realize that if I was too domineering, my squad would start to hate me, and chaos would happen. But at that point in my life, a combination of success and hormones was making me edgy. I was turning into quite the dragon lady. In fact, one of my more aggressive moments actually involved getting driven home by the police.

It all started with Mom coming into my room one day. She had a way of making me do things I really didn't want to do. This particular day she had that "Jennifer, God is calling" look on her face and asked if I would go on a "drive for charity."

What that amounted to was me taking a small can and walking through my neighborhood, knocking on every door and saying, "I'm collecting for muscular dystrophy;* would you like to contribute something?" It seems simple enough, but I made it much, much more complicated.

Collecting money for a charity was a little embarrassing for me. Every time a door would open I would feel a tingle creep up from behind my ears and spread onto my cheeks—which I knew at that moment were turning red as a rose. This feeling was worse at the houses where I knew the people. I could tell they were thinking, *Oh, here's Jill Wilson's daughter. Isn't that cute? She's collecting for charity.* The corners of my mouth would automatically curl into the rose-red cheeks.

"Hi, I'm on a muscular dystrophy drive," I'd begin, trying to straighten my lips out and look serious. Usually the person at the door immediately started digging around looking for loose change and dollar bills. I almost never had to finish my sentence. People in my neighborhood were generous.

Once the jar was half full, I started feeling pretty good—like I was helping some kid somewhere with a disease that they had no cure for. Embarrassing as it was, collecting for charity had good feelings that came along with the package. It promised to be a winner of a day—that is, until I got to Mrs. Underdown's house.

This was one woman whom I had never met. I knew nothing about her. Most of the houses on my block held people I either knew or my mom knew. Mom would chatter about them as we drove by, telling me they were on the school board or that they had kids in college or other things that I instantly forgot. Nothing had ever been said, however, about Mrs. Underdown. But I will *never* forget her.

Her door swung open and there she stood. "Hi, I'm collecting for muscular dystrophy and . . ." I started my speech, but my voice faded off. Mrs. Underdown was a thin woman with drab brown hair pulled back in a bun and wire-rimmed spectacles perched on her nose. She wore a boring gray dress, but more important, she wore a very sour expression on her face. Suddenly I missed all the adoring neighbors who thought I was cute. Mrs. Underdown obviously didn't think I was cute *at all*.

"I'm not interested," she snipped, turning her nose high into the air. Then, to my amazement, she shut the door in my face. I stood there in shock for a few seconds. *Oh, well, you can't win 'em all*, I thought. But then it hit me that her crime was much bigger than snubbing me. She was depriving innocent, sick children of a cure for a terrible disease. And she lived in a large house with a beautiful yard and two cars in the garage. She wasn't just cold and mean; she was stingy. My sense of justice had been terribly insulted. All I could think of was revenge.

God tells us that it's His job to take revenge on people, but I didn't know that part of the Bible yet. So I felt it was my Christian duty to somehow pay Mrs. Underdown back for slamming the door in my face, and in the faces of all those sick children. But the way to pay her back didn't occur to me until my friend Kate Shaw came visiting from Aurora.

Kate had grown up in a house full of boys—in fact, she was the only girl in a family of seven kids. Dealing with so many brothers had made her a pretty tough girl who wasn't afraid to get rowdy at times. This made her the perfect partner in the crime I wanted to commit.

"Let's take an egg and throw it at Mrs. Underdown's window," I proposed after explaining who she was and her outrageous behavior. Kate immediately felt the same sense of purpose I did, and we crept into the kitchen to secure the needed ammunition for our mission.

When we arrived at Mrs. Underdown's house the night was upon us, covering us with darkness as we slithered into her front yard. Standing near her window, I could hardly keep myself from giggling. There she sat in her chair reading a magazine with the same bun hairdo, the same wire-rimmed glasses, and the same sour look on her face. I stifled my laughs and took aim.

POW! The egg hit the picture window and gooped down the glass. If there had not been a window there, Mrs. Underdown would have had egg all over her bun. I couldn't have made a better shot. Kate and I scampered out into the night, our sides splitting with laughter.

Finally we calmed down and, after hiding out in the bushes for a few minutes, started our stroll home, slapping each other on the back and shouting in victory. That's when the police cruiser pulled up. Frozen in fear, we stared at the police officer who stuck his head out the window. "Girls, there has been some vandalism in the neighborhood. Do you know anything about it?"

I was amazed at two things. One, that Mrs. Underdown had actually called the police, and two, that the police didn't just *assume* that we had thrown the egg. It was then that I made the second bad decision of the night. Instead of telling the truth, I chose to cover up.

"Vandalism? No, I don't know anything about it," I said, with Kate chiming in. I don't think we were very convincing, but the officer went along with the program.

"OK, then, why don't you let me take you home? It may not be safe to be out here," he said. We really didn't feel threatened by egg-throwers, especially since we knew they were us, but we couldn't say no to a police officer. Like zombies, Kate and I got into the car and told him how to get to our house—only half a block away. Things went downhill from there. Once in the driveway, the officer didn't just let us out like I had hoped.

"Let me walk you to the door," he said, turning off his car. Then, instead of letting us go in by ourselves, he rang the doorbell. My dad answered the door. Dad was hard to shock, but I could see the surprise on his face as he took in the scene—his daughter, her friend, and a man with a badge.

"Mr. Wilson, Sergeant Sparks from the Bayside Police Department," he said, with dad nodding politely. "There seems to have been some vandalism in the neighborhood, and I just thought your daughter would be better off at home." As if he knew Dad wanted details, he continued. "Someone threw an egg at Mrs. Underdown's picture window."

If it had been something seriously destructive like bashing a car with a baseball bat or setting fire to a garage, Dad would have ruled me out. But as he envisioned the egg splatting the window, it seemed to be a crime tailor-made by his mischievous daughter. Knowing that the officer was trying in a tactful way to tell my dad that his daughter was the egg-throwing criminal, Dad took the plunge. He looked straight at me and asked, "Did you do it?"

"N . . . no," I stammered, lying through my teeth. A moment of silence followed, after which Sergeant Sparks excused himself and glided off in his cruiser, leaving me in the front hall with my dad, whose newspaper still hung from his hand, half-read.

"Did you do it?" Dad asked again, staring me down. I knew very well that any punishment the Bayside Police would administer for throwing eggs couldn't compare to one of dad's punishments.

"No!" I said, part insulted, part scared stiff, turning to head up the stairs. Once in my room, Kate and I sat on my bed and twiddled our thumbs. Somehow living with our lies was taking all the fun out of the evening. It was as though a dark cloud had come over us and settled, bringing cold, damp sadness. I started to feel very bad for what I had done, but I could see no way to come clean. Then the door opened and an angel walked into the room.

The angel was my mom. She had that "You really messed up but I love you anyway" look on her face. It was as if beams of mercy were shining out of her eyes as she sat down next to me on the bed. Bringing those eyes within inches of mine, she looked deep into my soul and asked, "Jennifer, did you do it?"

"Yes!" I blurted out along with a loud sob. Tears burst out of my eyes and flooded my face. I couldn't lie to my mom. After several minutes of comforting, she floated out of the room to tell my dad that I had confessed. I realized this when I heard Justice bellowing from the bottom of the stairs.

"Jennifer, come downstairs!" he shouted. "You call the police department right now and admit the whole thing."

"Oh, don't make her do that," Mercy pleaded.

"She has to!" Justice thundered. "She has to face what she did."

"But dear," Mercy cried, "she's really sorry. Don't be so hard on her."

And so Mercy and Justice argued over my fate. This particular evening Mercy triumphed over Justice, and the police department was never called. But I have a feeling that a certain Sergeant Sparks sat at his desk that night with a deep satisfaction in his soul, knowing that he had dealt very wisely with a naughty young woman.

Did I learn anything from the experience? Fortunately, I had more than egg yolk in my skull, and yes, I learned. I learned that revenge is not my job. Would I ever get in trouble again? Unfortunately, the worst was yet to come. I still had that edgy attitude that made me a few enemies on the cheerleading squad and in the neighborhood. But I never thought that attitude of rebellion would cause a problem so serious that the whole town would gasp in shock.

---

*A muscular disease that can cause the muscles to waste away, leaving a person disabled.

Chapter 7

There are some moments in your life that are freeze-framed in your memory. For me, one of them for me is the moment on a spring evening when my kid brother Scott threw my bedroom door open without knocking. This was a crime punishable by door slamming, which normally would have happened, except that what Scott said paralyzed me. He weighed about 75 pounds at the time (now he's up to 220), and his skinny little bare chest was inflated with excitement. His eyes were like two wide brown alarm clocks. Then he blurted out a declaration about Sue Cook's house.

Sue Cook and I had become best friends. We spent hours together dreaming up new ways to entertain ourselves—by playing "you eat it," for instance. "You eat it" was a game where one person took any three foods in Sue's kitchen, mixed them together, and the other person would have to eat it.

Have you ever tried orange soda mixed with spaghetti and mint jelly?

She has.

Have you ever tried maraschino cherries tossed with potato salad and Cheez Whiz?

I have.

You may have guessed that both Sue and I had a maximum of mischievousness with a minimum of supervision. Those two things are a deadly combination. Add to that the fact that we were not committed to God in any way, and you have a formula for disaster. So here it is in mathematical form. Mischievousness, minus supervision, minus God equals—well, you'll see what it equals in our case.

We were in eighth grade, and our hormones were cookin'. Kids generally become more risk-oriented and experimental when they hit their teens. That can be a good thing or a bad thing. It seemed that Sue and I raised this age-old phenomenon to new heights as we'd contemplate our day's activities. For example, there was a time we thought climbing roofs was a novel and worthy pursuit. We jumped off higher and higher points, sometimes using umbrellas, hoping we'd float. One Sunday we planned together.

"Let's go to Wendy's house and then go to the school and climb," Sue suggested. Wendy had become, of all things, one of my friends.

"No way. They'll catch us!" I said.

"Not today—it's Sunday. The janitors work on Saturday," she said. That was all the reassurance I needed. We ran one block to Wendy's house, then one block to the school. Wendy showed us how to hoist ourselves up using the windowsill, and soon all three of us were on top of the building. It was a flat roof, so we ran freely from one end of the school to the other, just enjoying the feeling of being on top of the world—or *our* world, anyway. It was our little secret view of Bayside Elementary. But actually it wasn't so secret, because the Bayside Elementary School roof was visible from the Bayside Police Station.

"Look! The cops!"

Wendy—who was the tallest and always seemed on the lookout for police—yelled the warning. Sure enough, a little black car was crawling up the school driveway.

"Here, slide down on the window awning," I yelled, as the three of us ran to the edge of the roof. Wendy was the first to ride down the slats, landing with a thud on the ground. Sue and I followed, and then the three of us disappeared into the woods.

One evening Sue and I decided we wanted to jump on a trampoline. The problem was that it belonged to someone else, namely Allen Schatz. Allen was a short, high-IQ kid with wire-rimmed glasses and a very bossy, loud mother. The other mothers tended to talk about her with such comments as "What a piece of work!" and "I can't believe she did that!" Mrs. Schatz was not a woman to be messed with.

"We can jump on Allen Schatz's tramp, but how are we going to avoid being seen by Mrs. Schatz?" I asked Sue.

"Just go after dark. I did it before and she never came out," she said. The problem was Sue alone wasn't as loud as Sue and Jennifer together. As we snuck into the Schatzes' yard and bounced, our giggling seeped into the walls of the house. Suddenly a short, round lady with a very poofy hairstyle stood next to us.

"THIS IS A PRIVATE TRAMPOLINE AND A PRIVATE YARD," she yelled—and boy, could she yell. Immediately Sue and I bounced off the tramp and hit the ground running before Mrs. Schatz could see who we were.

And so we lived our lives in a constant state of boundary-pushing and punishment-evading.

One of the things Sue and I did with our spare time was smoke cigarettes. I know, how dumb of us— but I have to be honest. This was especially bad given the fact that I had convinced my mother to quit smoking only about a year before.

"Mom, listen to this article about cancer," I had said.

After reading about one smoker's surgery in which his voice box and lower lip had to be cut off and he had to talk using a special voice-maker machine, Mom said, "You've convinced me. I'll quit."

"Really?" I said, impressed that I had that much power over my mom.

"Yes, really," she said. "I was thinking about it anyway, and your father has been urging me to quit, so this article that you've read is the last straw."

And now I was doing the very thing I had pressured her about. Sue's mother was a smoker and had all kinds of half-smoked cigarettes in the ashtrays around the house. We'd fish them out, straighten them, and light up. The nicotine made us feel fuzzy-headed for about one minute if we could quit coughing long enough to inhale.

One day when we were passing a cigarette back and forth between us, we heard the side door open and close. "What's that?" I asked, trying to hide the burning cigarette.

"Someone must be home," Sue whispered, equally paranoid. She stood up and tiptoed toward the door, calling softly, "Anyone home?" There was no answer. Meanwhile, I was so shaken that I dropped the burning cigarette between the cushion and the side of the couch. Sue came back to find me trying to retrieve it.

"It was only Heidi," she said, referring to her dog, which had somehow been given the ability to open the door.

"Sue, I dropped the cigarette!" I cried, still fumbling around. We found that it had burned its way through the cloth into the couch, where we couldn't possibly retrieve it.

"What should we do?" Sue asked.

"Let's pour some water on it," I said. And with that Sue ran to the kitchen twice, pouring glasses of water right on the little black hole the cigarette had left.

"Here, let's spray some Glade to kill the smell," she said, dousing the hole with spray deodorizer. She didn't see the little warning on the label: CAUTION! HIGHLY FLAMMABLE! After all, we weren't in the most intelligent state of mind. Finally we sat back and sighed with relief that we weren't caught.

"I'm supposed to go to a family picnic tonight," Sue told me, "so I have to leave now." She gave me a stern look. "Don't ever tell about this."

"OK, Sue," I said, and headed home on my bike.

That brings us to the moment when my brother Scott threw open my bedroom door and made his memorable announcement. A few hours had passed since I'd gotten home, and I was getting ready for bed. "Jennifer!" Scott had yelled. "Sue Cook's house is burning down!"

There was not a question in my mind as to what had started the fire. Propelled by intense guilt and fear, I raced to her house, riding my bike, then throwing it down to run the last few blocks until I reached the road where Sue lived. A mob of people choked the street and yard, but I could still see the black smoke billowing out of the windows. The house was brick, or it would have burned to the ground.

Someday I'm going to make enough money to pay these people back for burning their house down, I vowed, guilt-filled and terrified. I hated the feeling of being under a cloud of condemnation and debt. I just had to tell someone. The first person I confessed to was a skinny, brainy kid named Jim Rice. Jim, like so many others, was running toward the burning house. Desperately pulling in some breath, I blurted out the truth while Jim stared at me through coke-bottle-thick glasses as if he'd seen a ghost. "Jim, we did it! We started the fire! I know we did! Smoking!" I screeched.

He stared back at me without a word.

"I can't believe this happened!" I said. "I'm too young to have burned a house down!" Jim stared some more.

I ran to the backyard, where Sue was surrounded by a clique of girls. Putting my tear-stained face in hers, I looked her in the eye, begging without words for some comfort. I would have confessed right then and there to the police, the parents, and the PTA if Sue had given me the go-ahead. But no such release would I have.

"Don't tell anyone!" Sue hissed.

"How can I not tell anyone?" I whispered.

"You just can't tell anyone. My dad will kill me!" she said under her breath.

"Sue, how can we keep this secret?" I pleaded, but her glaring eyes told me that she wouldn't budge. How could I carry such a burden by myself? But how could I go against the wishes of my best friend whose house I had helped burn down? I was forced to choose between honesty and friendship, and I chose friendship. Somehow I couldn't cross Sue's will and risk losing her. We took the whole mess and pretended we didn't know a thing about it. There was talk about an electrical fire and a short in the wall. Who could tell how it started? House fires happen.

To complicate matters, Sue's parents were in the midst of a divorce. The fire took away their living space, and kind of moved the divorce along more quickly. Somehow, I always felt as if the fire *caused* the divorce, but that's because when there's divorce, kids tend to blame themselves.

Our plan worked for about a year. Sue's mom moved into the Holiday Inn for a while; then her mom and dad moved into separate houses, and Sue went back and forth between them. She began to attend a different school, but we stayed friends. Perhaps part of our bond was our common secret, and our common fear of discovery.

And yes, we got caught. Sue's dad was, of all things, a lawyer. One day he found a note I had written to Sue that revealed the whole matter. He arranged a meeting with Sue and I to discuss what would be done. Doomsday had arrived.

"So, girls, it seems that you were responsible for the fire. Is that so?" Mr. Cook inquired in a very businesslike, matter-of-fact tone. He had asked us to meet with him in the den, which was a cold room with a wood floor and wooden chairs. There were lots of windows, and the blinding sun glared in as if to expose every secret. Sue and I sat with our hands folded and our eyes cast down.

"Yes, we were responsible," Sue said, looking straight ahead.

"Jennifer, do your parents know about this?" Mr. Cook asked me.

"No, they don't," I said, dreading what he'd say next.

"I want you to tell them."

The verdict was in. I would tell my mom, which was like telling my parents, because my mom would tell my dad. It was that mercy/justice thing again. He'd freak out—and I can't say I blame him—and she'd soften the blow, which was seemingly her job.

But telling her was the hardest thing I have ever had to do. That's another freeze-framed moment in my memory. I call it The Confession. It was a cold, gray day. Mom and I were sitting in her station wagon after a trip to Brown Port Shopping Center. "Mom? Remember Cook's fire?" I whispered.

"Yes," Mom's eyes darted around in anticipation of bad news.

"I was responsible for it."

Ugh. I still feel sick thinking about how much pain those words brought.

"What do you mean, you were responsible for it?" she asked in disbelief.

"Well, Sue and I were smoking in the house, and dropped the cigarette into the couch. We poured water on it, but it lit—"

"You were *smoking?*" Mom asked as if there was a fog around her brain.

"Yes."

"After you persuaded me to *quit* smoking, you *started* smoking?" she asked. Mom had a talent for piercing my heart full of holes.

"Yeah, Mom. I'm really sorry."

What more was there to say? Her eyes had a beautiful softness to them, and when they filled with tears they were even prettier. But it sure hurt to see Mom so sad. My punishment was watching her cry. *Worse than the electric chair,* I thought.

Although her house and her parents' marriage were in ashes, my relationship with Sue survived the fire. Lasting friendships are so great! Unfortunately, Sue's mom decided to move to Arizona. That meant that Sue would live in another town with her dad for half of our ninth-grade year, then move out of the state to live with her mom. And *that* meant that I would have to face high school alone, without my best buddy.

Life had mixed a lot of things together and said, "You eat it." A house fire, separation from a friend, and a change in schools were not a very good-tasting mix. But the flavors were about to get a lot more subtle and complicated. Although I felt as if I'd had a very intense life already, high school would be even more exciting—and at times, even harder to swallow.

Chapter 8

Five elementary school districts spilled their graduates into one 2,500-student high school called Nicolet. Oprah Winfrey went to Nicolet for a while, but I don't know how she liked it. I sure didn't, not at first. Going from Bayside Elementary, where I was a popular eighth grader, to a huge mass of kids, where I was nobody, was like a pet parakeet getting lost in the Amazon jungle.

I had made other friends at Bayside, but as soon as we were submerged in a high school setting, things changed. Lots of kids in the school did drugs, and some of my previous friends—such as Wendy Potter—walked down that road. The problem with me and drugs was that I knew they killed brain cells, and I needed every brain cell I had. Plus I saw Wendy stoned once. She was laughing to herself, kind of having her own private party. I could only imagine how goofy I would act under the influence of drugs— I was goofy enough already.

"A lot of the kids in my school do drugs," I said to Sue as we talked on the phone one day.

"Mine, too," she said, "And my sister Linda smokes pot all the time. She takes her bag of pot and files it under 'P' in her filing cabinet."

"Wow, she's organized," I said. "Do you think you'll ever smoke pot?"

Sue had to think about that one. Finally she answered, "I don't think so. I have too much fun without it." And that's where Sue and I stood for the time being. We continued to pursue our natural high by engaging in all kinds of off-the-wall adventures.

One of our favorite inventions was the whale dance—so named because it made a person's body resemble the movements of a swimming whale. What this dance consisted of was a process of throwing one's body off balance, then retrieving balance while keeping the arms limp at the sides. It was best done with a flat, clueless expression on the face. Sue and I practiced the whale dance diligently before we demonstrated it in public. We were waiting for the perfect whale dancing venue to appear.

The urge first hit us at a huge inter-high school dance. A rock band was hired to play, and hundreds of teens, eager to make the teen scene, flooded the gym. They stood in little cliques all around, peering out at each other. The girls waited to be asked to dance, and once the boys finally worked up the courage the prettiest girls were out on the floor.

"Will you dance with me?" I mockingly asked Sue.

"Well, of course!" she replied in the same tone. "Shall we do the whale dance?"

I laughed as loud as I could, and shouted, "Yeah, the whale dance!"

Running out to the dance floor, Sue and I began our big-fish boogie. At first no one noticed, but gradually the little bunches of girls began to look our way, pointing and gasping.

"Two *girls* dancing together?"

"What are they doing?"

"Is that Jennifer Wilson and Sue Cook?"

"That figures!"

"They're totally manic!"

The more they freaked out, the more "whaley" our movements got. Sue and I just loved being publicly idiotic. For me, it was friendship at its finest to find a soul mate as creative as I, and to be so immersed in our schemes that we didn't care what people thought. As high school freshmen, we found that peer pressure was pretty much all-pervading. If you let it, it would control your every word, every fashion choice, and every social move. I was glad to find someone who would join with me in fighting the control freak of "cool." We defied cool by being as uncool as we could be. And that was utterly, totally, radically cool.

"Yeah! The whale dance!" I shouted.

Sue shared my joy. "I love the whale dance," she called out. And with that, we ran off the dance floor and out of the gym, laughing the whole way home. It was a perfect night.

I had two lives. One was ruling the weekend world with my best friend, Sue, and the other was being a weekday wallflower at my local high school. I was definitely lost in the shuffle of the masses of kids at Nicolet. However, one friend emerged from the situation. Tim Cleary rode my bus, and we shared a common passion for hobbits.

"Have you read this book?" he said one day as we rode between Brown Deer Road and Lake Drive. I looked at the pen-and-ink drawing on the cover and read the title: *Lord of the Rings*.

"No, I haven't read this. It looks like my kind of book, though."

"I challenge you to read it in a week," Tim said, holding it on its side to show a thick 500-plus-page volume. "Will you accept the challenge?"

And that began a relationship that was based on a mutual effort to bring hobbits and elves into our lives. In fact, after I had read the entire *Lord of the Rings* trilogy and had assumed the identity of a hobbit, Tim challenged me to graduate to elf status.

"If you can get from E wing, next to the library, to F wing, near the science rooms, in 10 seconds, I will dub you Elf Jennifer," he announced one day. The next day found me sprinting through the halls, trying to pass Tim's test.

We had found a little world we could escape to.

Life at Nicolet was cold, confusing, and, frankly, boring. Life in Middle Earth was full of wonder and mystery, and the line between good and evil was clear. At Nicolet, we had to watch our backs. In Middle Earth we had friends—Frodo, Bilbo, and Sam. At Nicolet we had an identity crisis. In Middle Earth we knew who we were—hobbits trying to graduate to elfhood.

As is often the case with boy/girl relationships, an attraction developed. It became obvious one day as Tim and I rode home. Things got tensely quiet for a moment, after which he said, "Will you go to homecoming with me?" Homecoming was a special dance that happened every year to celebrate football season. Not that either of us were into football, but the dance was a chance to court the girl you liked.

I almost swallowed my tongue. "Homecoming?" I gulped.

"Yeah, homecoming," he repeated.

I hadn't been sought after since Dennis McCabe chased me down the hall in sixth grade. It felt strange to think about Tim changing from a friend into a boyfriend. But to say no would be to hurt his feelings and trash our friendship. Even though I never told him, he was the only thing separating me from total aloneness. All of these thoughts went stampeding through my head, leaving only two little words in my mouth.

"Oh. Sure."

And that was it. To homecoming we would go. The night arrived in splendor as my mother put the finishing touches on a yellow gown she had sewed herself. Tim arrived at the door looking very fine in a tuxedo. He was too young to drive, so his dad was our chauffeur that night. Most of the dance we sat at a table of friends and made self-conscious small talk. When Tim finally walked me to the door, there was an awkward "Are we supposed to kiss?" moment that was quickly followed with a "No" moment.

"Thanks for a fun time," I said, and he was gone, never to return as the friend he once was. I hate it when that happens.

It's too bad that there was such pressure to become romantically involved. If it had been understood that friends could spend time together simply as friends, our relationship might not have taken the turn it did. But unfortunately I was scared off by the pressure to decide if I wanted him as a boyfriend or not.

After that, Tim's sentiments toward me shifted toward being a major tease. I was walking down the hall one day with a huge stack of books balanced on my head. Out of the river of hurrying students shot Tim from the other side of the hall. He had seen me carrying the books and considered it a golden opportunity.

WHAAAAMM! His arm shot out of nowhere and knocked my books into the air. As they splayed out all around me, students began to stumble over and tromp on them. I looked up to see from whence the arm had come. There was Tim's face, snickering gleefully. But it all seemed a little too serious.

Another time he got a group of three conspirators together to "string Jennifer up." We were on a field trip to a nature reserve. I saw the group coming toward me with Tim in front, and I immediately suspected a problem . . .

"Seize her!" Tim ordered, whereupon two of them grabbed my legs and the other my arms. I screamed at the top of my lungs, half-laughing, but half-wondering whether I'd survive whatever they planned to do. After escorting me to a nearby tree, Tim gave yet another command: "Who has the rope?"

Rope! I panicked. *What are they going to do with a rope?*

"Tie her feet!" Tim shouted, taking the rope from the hands of his accomplice and wrapping it several times around my legs. *At least it's not my neck*, I thought. Then Tim used his Boy Scout training and tied a huge, secure knot. Once my ankles were fixed tight, he flung the rope over a branch of the tree. "OK, let's string her up!" he yelled in triumph. The four of them pulled the rope and hoisted my body up until I was hanging upside down, like a bat with long blond hair.

"Hey, if you leave me here, you're in trouble," I yelled. I was half laughing, but only half. The other half was truly afraid being left dangling until my brains started to flow out of my ears. Fortunately, reason prevailed.

"OK, if she's gonna whine, then let her down,"

Tim ordered his thugs, untying his ultraknot. Then they lumbered off into the woods to hang with the grizzly bears. I was left sitting alone at the foot of the tree, rubbing my ankles and counting my blessings.

It's generally understood that boys pick on the girls they like. If that's the case, Tim must have liked me intensely. But somehow the aggressive approach didn't serve to increase my affection for him. It was too bad that we had to leave our little hobbit world, but the pressure for something more than a friendship—wherever that pressure had come from—had ruined ours.

Lonely again, I wandered the halls like a lost lamb. To add to the confusion, my former crush got cancer. Jim Lubotsky seemed healthy, but suddenly he was out of school for an operation. His twin, Tom, had to explain the situation to their friends. Stu later relayed it to me.

"They found cancer in Jim's eye. They're going to take out the tumor, and he should be fine."

"What about his eye?" I asked.

"He'll probably have a glass one," Stu said. And I thought, *glass eye or not, he'll still be cute.*

Jim returned to school with a black patch to cover the incision. He was his old, friendly self, and we all thought he'd pull through. But shortly after he returned, he stopped coming to school again. Then one day Stu came home from school with a hurt expression on his face. At dinner he announced to the family, "Jim Lubotsky died."

Mom was the first to react. "What? I thought his cancer had gone into remission."

Dad said, shocked, "He was so—young!"

I couldn't bring myself to respond. I just felt empty inside. How could someone whom I had conversations with at the very table where we were eating be . . . gone? Nonexistent? It just didn't compute.

The funeral was held at Jim's family's synagogue. It was packed wall-to-wall with kids who knew and loved Jim. After a very serious service full of Hebrew readings, it was announced that we would now walk to the nearby cemetery for the burial. A wide river of kids flowed down the perfect green grass toward the cemetery. An exact rectangle had been dug and roped off, the brown dirt piled up next to it. The sea of kids flowed around the rectangle, waiting for the casket.

I was facing Sue and Diane Harper, twin sisters who were friends with Stu and the Lubotskys. Normally they were chatty and giggly, but today they looked like lost children. A huge black car pulled up. It seemed like every kid watching was holding their breath. No one made a sound. The back of the hearse opened up, and the big casket was pushed out. A few cemetery employees fastened the casket to some cables that swung down from a big crane.

Grrrrrrr, the crane strained to lift the casket over the deep hole.

Every kid held their breath.

The casket was slowly lowered until it finally hit

the bottom of the rectangular hole with a thud.

At that moment Sue and Diane burst into hysterics. As soon as they broke the silence, the crowd let loose one long, loud group wail. Our friend Jim was in that box, and was about to be covered with brown earth and left there forever. Or so we thought.

When the burial was over, we left the cemetery and wandered back into our lives. It would be the same, minus one very special person, Jim Lubotsky. Was that really the end of Jim? Or was there a heaven for good people like him? Where did people go when they died? These questions pressed hard on me.

But a more dominant question was: Where did I belong in this high school? One group of kids did lots of drugs; another was very athletic. Then there were the studious types and the chains-and-leather types. Scattered all around these cliques like broken toys were the rejects that didn't fit in anywhere. That was me. Where did I belong? Since I wasn't fully listening to God's voice, I let someone else answer that question. His name was—*sigh*—Rick.

Chapter 9

Out of the 248 boys in my freshman class, there were a few that stood out. You know, Prince Charming types. The types that make little clusters of girls turn into a wall of whispers when they walk by. The types that always seem to be at the center of a movie screen, even when they're scratching behind their ears. The types who can wear anything well—even eye crispies.

Rick Kagen was one of these types. Dark-haired and buff, he walked the halls with confidence. For the entire first quarter of school he had a different girlfriend every week. One week he was seen hand in hand with Jerry Joslove, the girl who was becoming a pro dancer. The next week it was Dana Altman, the queen of the chic clique of girls who wore designer labels. Celia Atkins was next with her straight-A status and her wealthy parents. And the list went on. I tended to think of these beautiful people as a different species, a race of beings somehow separate from us run-of-the-mill types. I thought the worlds would never meet—the beautifuls were destined to live in isolation from others, lest they become forever tainted with averageness. And so I watched people like Rick from afar, never daring to cross the gulf.

But then he crossed the gulf to me.

"Hi, my name is Rick" were the first words from his lips that entered my universe. We were on a school-sponsored ski trip, chilling out in the lodge. A group of us were sitting by the fire eating our daily dose of junk food.

"Oh, I'm-uh-Jennifer." My voice came out in a semi-squeak, as if I was using it for the first time.

Without breaking eye contact, he said, "I've seen you around school, I think."

Oh? I thought, *Actually, I've seen you, too. But if I told you that I'd seen you with Jerry Joslove, Dana Altman, Celia Atkins, and countless others you'd think I was a stalker.*

"I've seen you around, too," I squeaked, wondering when he'd realize I wasn't good at talking to cute guys and say, "Well, I need to get going."

Not this guy. Not this time. He continued: "So, where are you from?"

"Well, originally, from Aurora, Ohio. But more recently, from Bayside." There! That sounded reasonably confident. Now that my voice was coming out in a normal tone, I could obsess over the way I looked. Were there any wads of spinach in my teeth? visible particles in my nostrils? noticeable earwax or facial hair issues? Come to think of it, though, how could I check, given that there was no mirror within eyeshot and what's more, Rick was still looking straight at me. I'd have to go with the flow.

"So you went to Bayside," he said. "Do you know Bill Pingry?"

Of course I know Bill Pingry, I thought. *He's another cutie who never so much as spoke a word to me. So why are you?* I wondered.

"Yeah, I know Bill," I said. "Or I know who he is."

He thought for a moment, and said, "What about Wendy Potter?"

Sure, Wendy! The girl who beat me up when I was 10.

"Yeah, I know Wendy," I said. "Wendy and I climbed our school roof and got chased by the police."

This prompted Rick to flash the most beautiful tartar-control Crest smile I have ever seen. Holding that smile as if his picture was being snapped, he said, "Well, since we know a lot of the same people, I think we can ski together."

In that moment the earth went into a holding pattern. Birds the world over paused in the midst of their birdcalls, and the wind stopped blowing. In fact, all nature bent low to observe the birth of the eighth wonder of the world—Jennifer being noticed by a good-looking guy. All modern transportation devices—cars, trucks, trains, boats, and planes—immediately stopped or had emergency landings. The New York Stock Exchange closed for the day, as did the White House and the Pentagon. Or so I felt.

"Sk-ski with you?" My voice was back to its squeak.

"Sure!" Rick said. *Where did he get that confidence, that energy, those teeth?*

"Oh!" *Such an intelligent answer!* "Umm." *Another moment of brilliance.* "Uhhhh." *National Honor Society, here I come!* "OK."

I'm sure the kids sitting around noticed as Rick and I made our way out of the lodge together. They probably whispered to each other and wondered about our relationship. Whatever they said or did, though, I didn't notice. I was too focused on trying to get my wits back so I could say something meaningful. What I finally realized was that Rick was a simple guy without one layer of phoniness, and that I could just be myself with him. We passed the warm, sunny afternoon skiing, chatting as we rode the chairlift. Since my snowplowing days with Benjy Wallace, I had become a good skier. Now I was finding out that I was a good talker. The weekend passed in uninterrupted social bliss. I was very suddenly launched from wallflower to superpopular girl status by the fact that I was seen with Rick Kagen. Popular people were now talking to me, whereas before they could have tripped over me and still managed to ignore my existence. Even on the bus ride home, I was welcomed into the elite-kids' section, which, before Rick, had been roped off by invisible cords of snobbery.

The crash came when we got back to Nicolet. It was then that the great masses of Rick's fans came out and swallowed him up. Once again, I was the wallflower and he the celebrity. He didn't make much of an effort to fight his way out and talk to me, so I figured he had lost interest.

My thoughts and feelings converged one day in algebra class. As the teacher talked about square roots, I wondered about love triangles. How could this be? It seemed as if Rick genuinely liked me. I wondered if there was a chance that he did. As I pondered, I made a small, white origami bird. Then I set the bird aside and, for the first time in many years, I prayed.

"Dear God. I haven't asked You for much because I'm not a very good person. But I'd like to ask You for one thing, and then I'll leave You alone. Please make Rick Kagen like me as much as I like him. Thanks, God. Amen."

As I left class that day, I noticed Rick in the hall. As usual, he was in the midst of a group of cool people, center stage, charming everyone's socks off. Somehow I found the boldness to walk straight into that group and stand next to him. He turned toward me with his photo-op smile.

"I have something for you," I said, holding up my origami bird. "Here."

It takes a pretty sensitive guy to receive a gift as gently as he did. He turned up his hand as I placed my little bird in it. As he tried to figure out what it was, I walked away. The little birdie would have to tell him anything more he wanted to know.

Two days later there was school assembly. Rick was outside the auditorium with his friends as I wandered through the door. To my utter shock, he followed me, asking, "Can I sit with you?"

"Sure," I said.

"Let's sit toward the back so we can talk," he said. My blood pressure rose about 400 points, but I tried to appear calm. As we sat down, he said, "I have something I need to tell you about."

And so the story spilled out.

"When I met you on the ski trip, I really liked you. But my conscience bothered me that whole weekend because I was already dating Marcy Curzon."

"You mean that girl over there?" I pointed to a petite girl with lacquer-shiny hair and big brown eyes.

"That's her," Rick said. "I knew we weren't going to last—I mean, Marcy is a nice girl, but she's more interested in the fashion scene than a real relationship. I didn't think she'd be hurt if I broke up with her."

"So you *broke up* with her?" I asked, somewhat horrified.

"Well, not exactly. I just told her about you, and we both kind of decided to go our separate ways. It really wasn't a big deal. She wasn't hurt or anything." It almost sounded like Rick couldn't live without a girlfriend, so he had just dated Marcy out of convenience.

"Well, I didn't mean to cause any inconvenience," I slowly said.

"You didn't." Rick gave me a look and said, "Jennifer, I've never been able to talk to a girl the way I talk to you. You're . . . you're *different.*" Considering how shallow most girls were, I took that as a compliment. "We both love nature, and we have the same values," he continued. "You care about people, and the world, and most girls I know care about their hair and their nails and having all the latest fashions." That was all Rick had to say to win me over. Our three-year relationship had begun.

For weeks afterward girls approached me in the hall.

"Are you dating Rick Kagen?" Jerry Joslove asked.

"I saw you with Rick. What's going on?" Dana Altman wanted to know.

"I heard you were going out with Rick Kagen," Celia Atkins said.

"Well, we've been seeing each other," I would say, laughing inside at the fact that they suddenly thought I was a real person.

There was so much that was right about this young romance, but so much that was wrong. They call it falling in love because when a person falls, they feel insecure. Romantic relationships are usually filled with fear, but somehow that fear becomes thrilling when it's mixed with mutual attraction. I won't lie and say that dating Rick wasn't thrilling—it was. But there's so much I would do differently now.

For a year and a half Rick and I spent every spare minute together. We didn't drive, so most of our dating involved riding our 10-speed bikes around the city, to parks, to concerts, and to friends' houses. The most hurtful part of our relationship wasn't so much the party lifestyle—although there were some bad choices made there—but rather the fact that we stuck to each other like Velcro, and pretty much forgot anyone else existed. Romance tends to absorb all your attention. You don't think you need anyone or anything else. Far, far too early in the game of my life a charming young man became my everything.

Then one day Everything left me with nothing. We were sitting in his yard, and his friends had just gone home. I was always more comfortable when they weren't around, because they didn't really like me. They thought I made Rick into a goody-goody. Well, apparently they finally convinced him that I was holding him back.

"Jennifer," he said with a distant look in his eye. This was not the Rick I knew. This was a stranger speaking. "I'm thinking it's time to get a break from us."

Of course my reaction was disbelief. I was still high on the falling-in-love endorphins. I still lived in a storybook world, and I didn't want to leave. I couldn't seem to convince him that this was *not* what he wanted.

"But Rick, we made future plans together."

"I know, but I'm not so sure now."

"Can't you just think about this for a while?"

"I have been thinking about it."

Finally I had to accept the fact that Rick was out of my life.

Reality crashed down on me hard. It felt like someone had ripped my heart out of my chest and left a big, bleeding hole. I had disconnected from my every friend in order to focus on Rick, and now that I needed a friend there was none. I didn't tell my parents, because they never approved of Rick to begin with. Sadness overwhelmed me until I couldn't eat or sleep much. I lost 10 pounds in two weeks. For the first time in my life I seriously considered whether there was a God or not. Is He the one that put this longing for love inside me? If so, could He fill it?

For several months I was alone with these questions. Then my situation improved when a set of new friends trickled into my life. The first was Ginny Tucker, a cute blue-eyed athlete with kinky blond hair who sat behind me in French class. Little did I know that she was watching the Rick drama unfold from a distance. She related to it because her boyfriend Kevin had broken her heart only a short time before. "Now here's a girl I know how to cheer up," she said to herself. And cheer me up she did.

"Hey, Nadia," Ginny whispered my French name in class one day.

"Oh, hi, Gabrielle," I replied.

"Have you ever been to Lake Park?" she asked,

"There's a great place to walk the beach."

"No, I don't have a car," I said, "and it's too far to ride my bike."

"I'll take you," she said. "Come to my house after school, how 'bout?"

Ginny and I never got to the park. After driving to her house, we yakked all afternoon while Ginny foraged around her house looking for food. Finally settling on a cooked, cold potato, she cut it up and ate it piece by piece while keeping a constant stream of conversation going. She told me all about Kevin and the breakup, and when I started to mope about Rick, she cut in with "Things will improve."

And they did improve. Ginny came with a package of really fun kids who were all a year older than I was. Because they all drove, we could go anywhere—skiing, rafting, partying—without adult supervision. Socially my life went from zero to 10.

And from a distance, Rick noticed.

Chapter 10

Why don't you take my horse for a ride some-
time?" Ginny asked me one warm spring day.
She owned a beautiful Appaloosa that she stabled
near a large park that was ideal for riding.

"I don't think I have the horse smarts to bridle
and saddle her by myself."

"Why don't you invite someone who is experienced to ride with you?" she asked with a twinkle in
her eye.

"Like who?" I twinkled back.

"Like Rick!" She laughed, knowing that Rick had
learned horsemanship at summer camp.

"I suppose I could," I said. "Thanks for the tip."

It was an idea whose time had come. Rick had
floated back into my life. Although he hadn't landed
on shore yet, he was realizing that his breakup with
me was more about pressure from friends than his
own feelings. He had hinted at spending time
together, but nothing came of it. At his next hint I
hinted back about the horse, and soon it was an offi-
cial date.

It was a golden afternoon. The earth was pushing flowers through the grass, and entire trees were decked out in pink and white blossoms. The horse carried us gently through paradise to the tune of hundreds of birdsongs. The lakes and streams shimmered with sunlight made into diamonds by the soft breeze. The emerald palace door was opened, and the royal trumpets blew. (OK, that last sentence isn't true, but it was at *least* as Disney as Cinderella.) I seriously wondered if maybe this was what heaven was like—beauty and love at the same time. There was a feeling of satisfaction in my heart, as if I had everything I wanted.

Unfortunately (or probably fortunately), my dad didn't want what I wanted. He had never really liked Rick's hair, his clothes, and his reputation as a wild child. He felt—as most dads would—that a careless young man was ruining his precious daughter's life. His grudge boiled over one summer night when Rick and I found ourselves outside the law.

It wasn't any federal offense, mind you. Rick and I loved nature, parks, and walking. On this particular night we decided to visit the bird sanctuary that was about midway between our two houses. The rub was that it had a big No Trespassing sign posted outside the wire fence.

"Should we go in?" I wondered. "It says 'No Trespassing,'"

"Sure!" Rick said.

As I thought about it, I felt myself getting bolder. "Hey, they trespassed on the Indians' land, and everyone trespassed on God's land. So how can they keep us out? This is *God's* bird sanctuary." Suddenly I had become very religious. With that, the two of us stashed our bikes in the bushes and made our way through the fence. We walked until it grew dark, then crossed the fence again and rode our bikes home. Other than trespassing, we had been very well behaved.

Unfortunately, the Bayside police were in no mood to congratulate us. I was halfway home when a police cruiser passed me and pulled over to the curb. When he jumped out and began walking my way I was sure he wanted some kind of help. Instead, our conversation was a typical cop-and-criminal cross-examination:

"Are you the owner of this bike?"

"Y-Yes."

"Was it hidden with another bike outside the bird sanctuary?"

"Y-Yes."

"Did you see the signs that read 'No Trespassing'?"

"Y-Yes."

"But you went in anyway?"

"Y-Yes."

"Get in the cruiser."

And with that the officer grabbed my bike, shoved it in his trunk, and opened the driver's-side door. *I might as well have been selling drugs or robbing banks the way this guy is treating me*, I thought. Directly in front of me was a rifle mounted on the dashboard. "What's this for?" I asked, feeling bold again. The officer remained quiet. He wasn't warming up to me any time soon. Just as with Sergeant Sparks after the egg-throwing fiasco, he escorted me to the door and spoke to my father.

"Mr. Wilson," he explained, "your daughter was trespassing in the bird sanctuary. I thought you should be apprised of the situation." With that he rode off into the night to nab more bird-sanctuary-invader types.

The moment the door clicked shut my father blew like a ring-o-fire volcano. All his feelings about Rick, which he had bottled up for years, came pouring out like hot lava in a long half-hour rant. "I don't like that boy!" Dad bellowed, "I don't like him at all! Not one bit! I don't like his hair. I don't like his clothes. I don't like his attitude or his reputation." Finally I threw my arms up in the air, screamed, and ran out of the kitchen into my room. Let's just say it was a night of high drama at the Wilson house.

At the time I thought my dad's anger was mean. Now I can see that it actually came straight out of love. Not that he did it perfectly. Blowing sky-high isn't recommended by family therapists. But there is a certain amount of healthy anger in true love. It isn't all soft, fuzzy, and oozy-goozy. Dad was right. My relationship with Rick, as good as it felt sometimes, wasn't really good for either of us.

The worst thing about a love that is based on feelings is that feelings change. I never thought it would happen, but as time passed, my heart stopped fluttering when Rick walked into the room. My nerves even got irritated when he said something dumb. Somehow he didn't seem as handsome, as intelligent, or as fun to be with. I started thinking about what I would do after high school. I was exploring new options and meeting new people. I was waking up to the fact that there was life after Rick.

And he noticed. We never officially broke up, but we slowly wandered away from each other. About a month after we stopped hanging out together, we talked briefly about how he was handling it. "Are you really hurting, Rick?" I asked, truly worried about him.

"I've lost my confidence," he said. "I feel so . . . *hurt.*"

I certainly knew what that hurt felt like. I had been equally wounded when Rick broke up with me. But revenge wasn't in my heart. His lips were quivering, and he put his hand on his mouth to make them stop. I tried to gently restore what confidence I could, but I finally had to walk away and leave him with God.

God. Who or what was God, anyway? The ultimate love, the love I thought would last forever, had dried up like a leaf and blown away. If that wasn't real, then what was? I started to ask very serious questions about life after death, about religion, and about why there was this big, dark, aching hole in my heart that never seemed to be filled.

I was convinced that I needed spiritual help. I sang in the church choir with my mom, but it just wasn't cutting it for me. It seemed as if the people worshipped the minister instead of God. One night I found out the hard way that the minister was just another messed-up human being. I was cruising around town with my friends, and we pulled up to a gas station. To my surprise, Reverend Shultz was standing at the pump.

"Well, hello, Reverend Shultz," I said as our eyes met. Strangely, instead of waving or saying hello back, he walked toward me quietly, taking my hand in his.

"You were always one of my favorites," he said, caressing my hand. My nostrils gave a red alert signal as the air between us grew saturated with the smell of alcohol. *He's drunk*, I thought, *and I don't like the way he's stroking my hand.* As soon as I could, I pulled away and took shelter in my friend's car, thinking, *Christianity must be a bunch of lies! Even the minister has a dark side no one knows about.*

Now that Christianity had been checked off my list, I decided to go religion-shopping and see if I could find the magic key. I thought maybe one of the other world religions I learned about in school had the answer. Around the city were several places that taught people about these ways of life. I mapped out a plan to visit them one by one and see what I could find.

The first stop on my journey was a small white house in the city. It looked like any other all-American house in an all-American neighborhood until a very hyper young man greeted me at the door. "Hi! My name is Brahma. You must be here for the meditation," he said. Brahma was wearing a white turban, white shirt, and white pants that looked like he had wrapped a bedsheet around his legs. I was instantly terrified that the sheet would come loose—but I hid it well.

"Hi, Brahma. My name is Jennifer, and I did come for the meditation," I said, but it seemed like Brahma didn't hear me. He made sweeping motions toward a little room off to the side of the front hallway. I obediently walked through the curtain that separated the room. There I saw about 10 people dressed like me, sitting quietly on the floor. There was a hush in the room, and a strange, sweet odor in the air.

Brahma stood just outside the curtain and swept a few more people in. Finally he announced, "The master is coming." I didn't have to wonder who the master was for very long. A very intense-looking man in white clothes and turban walked into the room and sat on a cushion at the front. He crossed his bare feet and looked over the top of all of our heads. His piercing blue eyes were very serious as he spoke through a long beard. "Today we will be doing some kundalini yoga exercises. Our first step is to tune in. This will set and calm your mind, and open you to guidance. Repeat with me, *'Ong nam guru dev namo,'*" he said. I solemnly repeated the strange words, wondering what in the world they meant.

Over the next hour we chanted, breathed, did deep knee bends, and all kinds of other exercises that made gym class seem like a walk in the park. When we were finally done, the master began to talk in a low voice that sounded as if he was trying to imitate a bullfrog. While he spoke about things like prana, mudras, and being healthy, happy, and holy, his blue eyes kept rolling back into his head. It reminded me of when my little sister had convulsions and Dad had to put her in an ice-cold bath to take her fever down. A combination of the weird atmosphere in the room, the strange eye-rolling of masterman, and the fear of unraveling sheet-pants gave me a totally creeped-out feeling—but I was so tired from the deep knee bends that all I could do was sit and stare.

Needless to say, I didn't find God that day. Nor the next, nor the next. Finally someone gave me a booklet that listed all the places a person could go to find enlightenment through meditation. "I'm going to go to one of these places to live. I don't care what my parents say. I just have to find the truth," I said, opening the book.

Each page had a description of the place and a picture of the leader, called a guru. On the first page

I saw a picture of a very fat man with a big belly sitting cross-legged. He wore nothing except for a cloth about the size of a narrow bikini. "I'm not going *there,*" I said to myself. The next place's guru was twisted up like a human pretzel. "Not there, either," I said. Next was a man with a beard down to the floor and a long white robe. "Nope," I said. Finally, there was a picture with a man so skinny that his stomach sank in like a human salad bowl. "I could eat my Cheerios out of that!" I cried, slamming the book shut. "I'm weird, but I'm not this weird. I'll just have to find God on my own."

One religion after another—Hinduism, Buddhism, Taoism, Jewish mysticism, Shamanism, this ism and that ism—got checked off my list. I thought maybe psychology had the answer, so I studied dream therapy, scream therapy, and whipped cream therapy (I'm kidding about that last one, but *not* the first two). You would think that for all the effort, the hole in my heart would fill up *just a little*. But if anything, it got bigger, emptier, and achier.

And I still had no idea who God was. Was He the God of the Christian Bible? Was He Jesus? Maybe She was a goddess of some kind. Or was "It" a mass of energy, like "the force," that just kind of seeps into everything? If God was just a personless force field, then why did I have lonely feelings? Why did I *need* God to be a person who could love me?

One night I decided to take a walk down a country road to think over my situation. As I trudged along, I got very real with myself. I said, "Self, you're out of answers. Nothing you've tried has worked. What's next?" The sky above me was an infinite, blue-black lake, like the dark hole inside me that seemed to go on forever. But I saw little white stars winking down at me as if someone up there was smiling. Suddenly a voice came—not a voice I could hear, but a voice I could feel. It said only three words:

"I forgive you."

Those three little words came shooting out of the sky straight into my heart. They told me everything I needed to know. God was a person after all. And I was a sinner who had hurt Him and others. But best of all, He freely poured out His mercy and forgiveness upon me.

I walked through the front door of my house and crept up to my room. I fell to my knees and prayed over and over, "Jesus, take me back to the Father." Somehow I knew that all my efforts to get back to God had come to nothing, but that in Jesus, God had come down to me and closed the big gulf between us.

As I sat in my dark little room, the big, achy hole in my heart began to fill. It felt as if warm soup was being poured into the empty belly of a starving child. The love that I had tried to find in friends, talents, popularity, boyfriends, and in exotic religions had finally arrived. As I walked out of my room that day I knew my life would never be the same. I was now a believer in Jesus Christ.

Could I keep quiet about my faith? Can a dog keep from barking when the mail carrier comes? Within a few days every person I knew—including the mail carrier—had heard about my belief in Jesus. One by one, I sought out my friends with my Bible open in my hand. "Hey!" I'd say, "listen to what I learned today." Reading out loud, I would hope for a flicker of interest. A few of them thanked me, but most of them looked at me as if I had grown a spare head. One friend cursed at me like a demon and never spoke to me again. Another told me in a mocking voice that she had a dream that I ate my Bible. It was a good thing I wasn't concerned about being Miss Popular, because I was very quickly demoted to Miss Loser.

In a way, I did eat my Bible, as in I absorbed it into my heart. In just a few months I learned lots of new things. After hitchhiking around the city to find a church, I met Seventh-day Adventists. They understood the Bible better than any other Christians I had met. I went to their Bible studies and church services, and learned more about Jesus. Finally I was baptized with nine other young women. That was the day I became a full-fledged Seventh-day Adventist Christian.

I wanted a lot of things out of life—cool friends, wacky adventures, fun times, sparkling success—but the most intense craving, the one under the deep layers of my heart, was love. That craving was planted by God Himself.

A lot of crazy things happened on my journey toward that love. I got beat up, went steady, acted in plays, cheered and cartwheeled, threw eggs, burned a house down, and experienced teen romance. Little did I know that at the end of the road stood Jesus, waiting for me to run out of ideas and run into His open arms.